CHRISTMAKER

CHRISTMAKER

A Life of John the Baptist

•

James F. McGrath

WILLIAM B. EERDMANS PUBLISHING COMPANY
GRAND RAPIDS, MICHIGAN

Wm. B. Eerdmans Publishing Co.
4035 Park East Court SE, Grand Rapids, Michigan 49546
www.eerdmans.com

Book design by Lydia Hall

Printed in the United States of America

30 29 28 27 26 25 24   1 2 3 4 5 6 7

ISBN 978-0-8028-8400-8

Library of Congress Cataloging-in-Publication Data

A catalog record for this book is available from the Library of Congress.

Unless otherwise noted, Scripture quotations are taken from the New Revised
Standard Version, Updated Edition.

Contents

Preface

This biography of John the Baptist was able to be written thanks to a sabbatical from Butler University in Indianapolis where I teach. This was my
first ever full-year sabbatical, the standard being one semester. After teaching
through the pandemic, I felt I needed a change of pace for more than one
semester if I was to return to teaching refreshed and reinvigorated. Equally important was my sense that this project deserved a full year of my undivided attention. I spent the sabbatical writing two books, both about John the Baptist.
In the past, I have tried either to make my scholarly books somewhat accessible
or to fill my popular writing chock-full of information that I felt was important
to support my claims. Per Murphy's Law, I suspect that neither academics nor a
general audience felt that I was truly writing what they wanted. This time, I decided to write for these two audiences separately. The academic monograph
bears the title *John of History, Baptist of Faith*, and in it, you can find a detailed
defense of many of the conclusions explored in the volume you hold in your
hands. This book, *Christmaker*, offers a life of John the Baptist, a biography.
That is something that others in the past have said cannot be written. I knew
it was possible and wanted to tell the full sweep of John's story as a biography
to provide the big picture, as well as dig into the details so that anyone who
wonders what the basis is for my claims in the relevant ancient evidence and
modern scholarship will have it. It is my hope that those who are interested
in both will read both, and that those who mainly want the biography but are
curious about the details will at least borrow the academic book from a local
library and dive into it in places.

The full-year sabbatical in itself, and the ability to spend it in multiple interesting locations, was made possible by a range of opportunities. My home institution, Butler University, provided me not only with the sabbatical leave and a great deal of library support but also a grant to allow me to spend summer 2022 in the Holy Land visiting sites related to John the Baptist, whether in historical reality or according to later tradition. The stories of those places and of some of the people I met are woven throughout the book. Whether mentioned in stories and anecdotes or not in the following pages, they deserve the kind of profuse thanks that prefaces are designed for. These include Shimon Gibson in Jerusalem (author of *The Cave of John the Baptist*), Achia Kohn-Tavor, who showed me around Tel Shalem, and Abood Cohen, my guide in Samaria. I am also grateful to my wife, Elena, and our niece Dana, who quite literally came along for the ride as I rented a car and drove myself around the Holy Land for the first time, including on obscure and twisty roads to places off the beaten path.

I had more conversations with academics and a wider interested audience over the course of the past several years than I can ever hope to mention individually by name. I nevertheless attempt to do so in the academic book, the appropriate place for full references and footnotes. Here I must nonetheless emphasize that all the thanks I offer in *John of History, Baptist of Faith* applies to the present volume as well, as this was one research endeavor with two products rather than two separate undertakings. Some of the places and the people associated with them must nonetheless be included here. I spent most of the first semester of my sabbatical as Visiting Fellow at Magdalen College and Sassoon Fellow at the Bodleian Libraries at Oxford University in England. This provided a context in which it really felt like all I should be doing is reading and writing, and then occasionally enjoying the many opportunities for conversations in the vibrant academic community there. The New Testament Seminar at Oxford University welcomed me and provided such opportunities. The Visiting Scholars Center at the Bodleian gave me a chance to give a talk with an accompanying display of rare manuscripts that I was spending time working with. Magdalen College afforded me an opportunity to give a public lecture and get feedback on some of my ideas. So too did the Center for the Study of Christian Origins at the University of Edinburgh. Durham University also honored me with the title of visiting professor, and the New Testament Seminar there invited me to deliver a paper on my research. All of these opportunities for feedback and discussion were immensely helpful. My spring semester was spent as the Newell Visiting Scholar at Georgia College and State University, which provided the opportunity to continue work on the book while teaching only one course (on the subject of women in early Christianity). The library there provided me with so many interlibrary loans that I never had to feel as though I was missing access to specialist collections related to John the Baptist (which is not a major focus at Georgia College). The Durham Residential Research Library provided an opportunity to finish off the sabbatical project back in the United Kingdom under the auspices of a Barker Fellowship.

I am grateful to Wm. B. Eerdmans Publishing Company for their enthusiasm for this project, and to BBH Literary for helping me craft the proposal and find just the right tone to genuinely connect the fruit of my research with anyone who might be interested. Even when academics intend to write for a general audience, we do not always do a good job of it, and so I know that credit is due to them for feedback and input. I am also grateful to the Mandaean community for maintaining their traditions as a living witness to one of the movements that John inspired. Finally, I must thank my wife, Elena, once again for reading a draft of each chapter and providing feedback. Add to that her willingness to support my dedicating a full-year sabbatical to this project, and it should be clear that there is no one else to whom it would be more appropriate to dedicate this book.

Introduction

Everybody thinks they know John the Baptist. He has good name recognition. There are at least a couple of things he is famous for that most people can rattle off. Yet I bet most readers of this book know him the way they know a homeless man they pass on their way to work each day, or a teller who tallies up the cost of their groceries every week at the supermarket. If the individuals in question suddenly disappeared and you were asked to describe them, where you thought there was familiarity, you would instead find an astonishing lack of detail, little apart from vague impressions. John is like that and yet different in at least one important respect. While every human being is inherently deserving of our respect, and our full attention when we interact with them, John the Baptist is someone who deserves to be not merely familiar but famous, for reasons that this book will explore. He presents the classic case of someone you would expect to be famous in their own right, yet who has been almost completely overshadowed by those who followed after him—even by individuals and traditions that explicitly give John credit for influencing them.

Our comparison to a homeless man was not chosen at random. Whether you have encountered John in stories in the Bible, in paintings, or in movies, you have probably been given the impression of John as someone who looked like something of a mess. For modern people, all you have to do is say that John ate locusts, and they will immediately envisage an unhinged bug-eating vagrant. Add to that the camel-hair clothing, and it cements the impression. If you have seen movies and television shows in which John is a character, his hair seems to become more wild and unkempt every time a new one is made. As it turns out, John's hair will prove to be very important to his story. His clothing, on the other hand, is something that traditional artwork and on-screen depictions get badly wrong. Admit it—you probably have the impression that John dressed like a caveman. Paintings and cinematic depictions might lead you to think that John had wrestled a camel to death, torn off its hide with his bare hands, and casually wrapped it about himself. John's clothing was not at all like that. Clothing from camel hair was rougher and less luxurious than that made from other types of fabric, but it was clothing. Indeed, you can still get yourself a camel-hair suit today (although, to be clear, I am not suggesting that John the Baptist wore one of those). John would not have been the only person wearing clothing from such material in his time. It was the fact that he wore it consistently—especially as the son of a priest, who could have dressed in something more comfortable—that made it striking. Add the leather belt, and it became clear to his contemporaries that John was essentially engaging in what we today might call cosplay.

John's clothing was reminiscent of what the prophet Elijah had worn (2 Kings 1:8). By dressing as he did, John styled himself as a prophet in the vein of those who shake things up, challenge the status quo, and even bring about regime change. John had the attention of political and religious leaders. According to Acts 19:1–7, he had followers as far away as Ephesus. This was no recluse, no street-corner oddball that people might be inclined to avoid. This was someone who was taken very seriously, on whose every word many people hung.

So perhaps we don't know John as well as we think. The reason people today are even aware of John is one that would have been unimaginable in his own lifetime. We know John because of Jesus. Equally unfathomable for most people alive today is that when John and Jesus were contemporaries, Jesus was known through his association with John. We are provided many indications of this in early Christian literature. At the beginning of the Gospel of Luke, the author tells his patron Theophilus that he has thoroughly researched the momentous events that had recently unfolded and wishes to present him with an orderly account of it all. He then starts not with Jesus, or even with Jesus's parents, but with Zechariah and Elizabeth and their son John. Toward the end of the Gospel of Mark (Mark 11:27–33), when religious leaders challenge Jesus and ask by what authority he does such things as driving out money changers and sellers of animals from the temple, Jesus responds by asking them about

John's authority and the source of his baptism. Jesus and John were linked, not just in the minds of their opponents and of early Christian authors but apparently also in the mind of Jesus himself. When we consider this, we realize that in our tendency to rush past John on the way to Jesus, we have made two mistakes. On the one hand, we have failed to pay adequate attention to someone who had a profound influence on Jesus. If we do not understand John correctly, we will misunderstand Jesus as well. On the other hand, we have missed an opportunity to allow what we know about Jesus to fill in our portrait of his mentor and thereby understand both better.

Because John's authority and activity were so important to Jesus and so central to his sense of his own identity and mission, what Jesus said and did provide important clues about what John said and did. Of course, the New Testament Gospel of John depicts the Baptist as suggesting that all attention ought to come to focus on Jesus (John 1:15, 27, 29, 34; 3:30). Scholars understandably suspect that those texts tell us more about what the gospel author thought the relationship between the Baptist and Jesus ought to be than about what John the Baptist actually said. Yet our earliest sources depict John as talking about someone who would come after him, who would be stronger than he (Mark 1:7–8). A central question that this book answers is how an individual whose contemporaries thought he himself might be the Christ (Luke 3:15) came to be thought of exclusively as the forerunner—or as we put it in the title of this book, the Christmaker.

THE SPLASH JOHN MADE

In summer 2022, I took a trip to Israel focused on visiting sites associated with John the Baptist. At the start of the trip, I stayed near a place in Galilee called Yardenit. Now, to be clear, this is not a site that is fascinating because it has an ancient association with John. The site was created relatively recently by a local kibbutz, near where the Jordan River leaves the southern end of Lake Tiberias or Kinneret (better known to many as the Sea of Galilee, a name given to it by the author of the Gospel of Mark). When the traditional site that Christians revered as the place John baptized Jesus was closed, inaccessible due to tensions between Jordan and Israel, the kibbutz created this site as an alternative for pilgrims. It has everything necessary: multiple separate sets of steps down into the river, with handrails; a changing room that you can use for a price; and a large gift shop full of the kinds of souvenirs that those who get baptized might want to have as a memento. Precisely because it is not a site associated with John either by scholars or by tradition, its popularity helps illustrate the interesting way that places come to have significance as pilgrimage destinations. Choosing locations that can help those who visit imagine and see themselves in ancient stories is something ancient people did and, at least occasionally, modern people do as well. This process at times preserves historical memory, while at other times it obscures it. The Gospels do not tell us where John baptized Jesus. A number of sites are mentioned in connection with John's activity. The wilderness is one. The term used does not specify the Judean desert or arid terrain in general, but merely places John away from large urban-population centers. According to Luke 3:3, John was active throughout all the region of the Jordan River. The Gospel of John specifically mentions Bethany beyond Jordan (1:28) and Aenon near Salim (3:23). The former location is somewhat obscure, but tradition identifies it with the classic pilgrim destination for those seeking the place of Jesus's baptism, the one whose inaccessibility led to the creation of Yardenit's alternative. People want a sense of connection with these stories and are willing to accept substitutes when necessary. After all, if you can never step in the same river twice, then going to and even entering the Jordan River anywhere will not make a physical connection with John and Jesus, even one mediated by water. It is the symbolism of the location and the connection with story that make places significant.

Already on the first day of that trip to Israel, diverse threads that I planned to weave together in this book began intersecting not only in my mind but also through social media. A Mandaean friend who lives in Australia saw that I was at Yardenit and asked whether it would be possible to conduct a Mandaean baptism there. I will tell you more about the Mandaeans at various points in the book, but for readers who've never heard of them, I want to briefly introduce them here. The Mandaeans are the last ancient gnostic group that has persisted all the way down to the present day. They hold John the Baptist in high esteem, but they are not fans of Jesus. You can see why their interest in Yardenit would potentially be puzzling. Since the site is not run by Christians, even though it is marketed to Christians, I cannot imagine there is anyone who would say no. Some Christians there at the same time might object, on the other hand, if they knew what Mandaean texts have to say about Jesus and in particular their very different version of the story in which John baptized him. In their account, John is hesitant to baptize Jesus not because John considers himself unworthy but because he believes that Jesus is trouble, someone who is misleading people and drawing them away from the truth of John's own teaching and practice!

The first time I visited Yardenit, a member of the group I was leading came prepared with empty soft-drink bottles so they could take some water from the Jordan River home with them. Their father was a Baptist minister and would add the water to his church's baptismal pool. Others have come with me to Qasr Al-Yahud, on the Israeli side of the river just across from the traditional site of Jesus's baptism by John in neighboring Jordan. Occasionally students have even decided to get baptized while there. Let me make a few things clear about that. These were students on a trip from a secular university, in which, of course, many of the students are religious. None of the students in question told me beforehand that they intended to get in the water. On one trip, three students suddenly showed up on the banks of the Jordan in white robes. My first thought was that they had planned this ahead of time without telling me, but I soon learned that wasn't the case. They had decided together on the spur of the moment to purchase the white robes from the shop located on the site. That little shop is there precisely to sell such baptismal accoutrements to those who wish to fully immerse themselves in the experience of visiting the Jordan River in the literal as well as the metaphorical sense. These were students from churches the theologies of which all say that one should be baptized only once. Yet they all had the desire to do so again. There is, it would seem, an instinct about baptism that runs counter to the theologies Christians espouse.[1]

The early church wrestled with the implications of baptism being a singular event and what happened in the case of someone who sinned after being baptized. The Mandaeans, on the other hand, have a baptismal practice that is explicitly and emphatically not a once-and-for-all event. Might the Mandaeans have preserved a practice closer to that of John? The Mandaeans esteem John as an ancient adherent and proponent of their religion. One does not have to be persuaded there was a historical connection between John and the Mandae-

---

1. The students on my trip have tended to be Protestant. There is a more official parallel in the renewal of baptismal vows at Epiphany in the Eastern Orthodox tradition, a ceremony in which many immerse themselves or are at least splashed with water from a river.

ans to recognize that their practice of repeated immersion raises an interesting alternative possibility about John's baptism, one that may be missed by those who approach it through the lens of Christian practices. Christians differ in the mode (e.g., sprinkling versus full immersion) but agree on baptism being a thing you do (or have done to you) only once. Yet as I have shared, there may be a deeper instinct that baptism could and should be understood differently. Historically, the church wrestled for centuries with the subject of forgiveness for postbaptismal sin. If Christians took a repeated rite for the forgiveness of sins and adapted it into a once-and-for-all identification with Jesus, then we can understand how this issue arose.

So many who visit the Jordan River have a desire to connect with that moment in the story of Jesus, to connect their own baptism symbolically and geographically with Jesus's baptism. The fact that Jesus was baptized is one of the ways we know that Jesus was part of John's movement, that Jesus embraced John's teaching and his ritual. The meaning of the historical event is thus quite different from its significance for Christians today. Indeed, the very fact that Jesus underwent John's baptism for the forgiveness of sins has been a conundrum for Christian theologians and other Bible interpreters almost ever since it happened. Such theologically awkward moments are crucial evidence for historians, who feel able to have confidence in what is described precisely because they feel certain the ancient Christian authors who record them would not have invented them.

Yet despite such anchors in history, the portraits of John by historians have differed significantly, in addition to (as we have already seen) the popular impression of John being badly skewed. Just as has happened with Jesus and other figures, conflicting information about John in our sources gets forced together into a single portrait that does not depict him in precisely the manner any of those sources does, and these portraits can vary widely. Some details are included at the expense of others. In other instances, sources that are in tension with one another are harmonized to produce a result that constitutes a third portrait unlike any of those on which it was based. In the past, the dominant approach to reconstructing the life of an ancient individual was to sift through the sayings attributed to them and stories about them, looking for tiny morsels that could be proven with a high degree of certainty to be authentic. In many cases, from the vantage point of modern historians looking back across the millennia, such rare tidbits of reliable information were few and far between.

Historians and other scholars would then try to arrange those into a portrait, like pieces of a puzzle, most of which was missing. Between the many possible ways of arranging those few pieces and the still more numerous possibilities for filling in the gaps between them, it is no surprise that countless reconstructions emerged that were radically different from one another. Some have responded to this situation by giving up on the quest for the historical Jesus and similar endeavors. That is where we ended up with respect to Jesus, even though multiple authors within a century of his death focused whole works on his life and teaching. If this frustrating and disappointing result was possible in the case of the historical Jesus, it might seem as though any hope of reaching the historical John the Baptist must be pure fantasy.

That might indeed seem to be the situation, were it not for the fact that historians have found a better way of approaching ancient historical figures. The effort to bring the past into focus depends on human memory. Almost no one in ancient times walked around with something like paper and pen, writing things down as they occurred. People wrote later, whether a few days or a few decades after the events transpired. Their memory was the mediator. Studies of memory have demonstrated the human capacity both to remember and preserve but also to forget and reimagine. When we do remember, however, one thing is clear. It is the *gist* of what happened and what was said that we remember best.[2] Even when specific details are forgotten, the overall impression remains. As it turns out, this is good news for what we are doing here. John the Baptist created a lot of ripples. Many suspect that those who wrote about him—Christians, the Jewish historian Josephus, the Mandaeans, and others—each had a desire to co-opt him for particular ends. Undoubtedly they did; and that is precisely what has long worried historians in the case of Jesus, too. The gist of John the Baptist, however, is far more likely to be discernible as we look at the ripples he caused and trace them back toward their source.

The older approach focused almost exclusively on our earliest sources of information about John: the New Testament Gospels and the historian Flavius Josephus. When we have early sources, they most certainly ought to be prioritized, all other things being equal. Later sources must be used with caution, since the passing of time and changing of context can lead to revisions

---

2. This point has been emphasized in particular by Dale C. Allison in his *Constructing Jesus: Memory, Imagination, and History* (Grand Rapids: Baker, 2010), 11–12.

and reinterpretations. Yet for those seeking to triangulate back on a historical impact, those later ripples can often still help us find the source, identify the moment of impact, and bring it into sharper focus. Even when it comes to later storytelling about John that is probably entirely legendary, so much of the material has received scant attention. There are manuscripts of ancient works about him that have not been translated or published. Instead they languish in libraries. Some have been published but only once, more than a century ago, or in an obscure journal article, none of which led others to pay attention to the text in question.

Thus there are many senses in which it is true to say that there is a lot we don't know about John the Baptist. Whether we are talking about apocryphal tales and sermons from centuries later, or the conclusions of historians about our earliest sources, a great deal of what can be known is not *widely* known. Hence one of the aims of this book is to introduce readers to those stories. Even the things that do not tell us about the historical John may tell us about his longer-term impact, just as is true of the abundant stories about Jesus that continued to be told and created in the centuries after his time. Even John the legend is largely unknown in our time; never mind John as a historical figure, which is the main focus of this book.

JOURNEYING WITH JOHN

In the pages of this book, I will take you on a journey that will introduce you to how much more has been written about John the Baptist than you've ever heard about. More of the legends (both early and late) contain at least a faint echo of the voice of the historical John than has hitherto been acknowledged. Some of what is familiar tells us much, much more about John than anyone has realized. This is due at least in part to the relative neglect of John as a focus of study in his own right. John hasn't been given the sustained and detailed attention he deserves. He has been overshadowed by Jesus, his former disciple and associate. If you are interested in John for his own sake, you will find this book fascinating. If your interest is mainly in Jesus, you will find that he appears regularly in the pages of this book and is himself an important source about his former mentor. You will also find that bringing John into clearer focus helps us understand Jesus—as well as Judaism, Christianity, Gnosticism, Islam, and many other traditions that branch off from him and reflect his influence. No other figure has made so many ripples that continue to reverberate in the present, if often in traditions that focus on someone other than John.

Here's what you will find in the chapters that follow. In the chapter "A Rebellious Son," we will explore the stories that tell us John was the son of a priest. When we encounter him as an adult, he has not followed in his father's footsteps and seems to be actively working to undermine the institution that his father is associated with. What turns a child in an establishment family into an antiestablishment rebel and activist? Neglected clues in the stories about John's parents and childhood allow us to fill in this part of our portrait with surprising clarity.

In "I Will Destroy This Temple," we explore how John came to invent baptism and what made his baptism stand out in an era in which immersion for purity as well as for pleasure was very common. We will also see that John did not leave merely implicit the fact that his baptism was a challenge to the temple. An incident in the Gospels connects directly with what other ancient sources tell us about John and leads to the surprising conclusion that something Jesus did may have led directly to John's imprisonment.

In "The Lost Sheep of Israel," we explore how John's activity in rural areas and locations far from Jerusalem put him in contact with diverse groups, including some that had never embraced the monotheism and Scripture that otherwise came to characterize Judaism. John's proclamation of a vision for all Israel, not dominated by a focus on one tribe or region, resonated with them and brought them out of the shadows. Some of their ideas influenced John, but they also held views that John would not have embraced. Thus we can explain how John's message and activity led to the emergence of Gnosticism. John also turns out to be an influence on the more mainstream growth of expectations in his era that God would intervene in history to restore his people Israel to their former glory, and on some famous individuals who each hoped that he might be the one to make that happen. Here John's role as Christmaker comes into clearer focus, as we also see clearly that John outlined a program rather than pointing to a specific person. More than one member of his movement hoped that he might be the "one who is to come."

In "Someone Is Coming," we dig further into what John and his followers expected and hoped for. John's references to "one who is to come" were understood by most to predict a royal figure who would be a complement to his priestly one. Some thought John was speaking about himself, but most expected there would be a second figure. Since "someone" or "a person" in Aramaic is "son of man," it is likely that Jesus's sayings about a coming son of man are a continuation of what John said. This chapter also explores how baptism invited people to have a mystical experience of spiritual rebirth and not merely to experience forgiveness.

"The Last Days" focuses on what we can learn about John from his most famous disciple, Jesus of Nazareth. Our various sources provide a fairly clear and consistent picture of John's emphases. His teaching focused on social and economic justice, but we also have information about his prayers. John taught in parables and puns that influenced the form as well as the content of Jesus's own teaching. This chapter also explores how Jesus went from being part of John's movement to the center of attention in what would eventually become Christianity, and how others of John's followers made brief appearances on the historical stage because they believed that they rather than Jesus were the ones to fulfill what John had predicted.

In our final chapter, "No One Is Greater Than John," we trace the threads beyond the lifetime of John in an attempt to make clear just how influential John was and remains. John's impact goes beyond those traditions that explicitly or implicitly indicate their indebtedness to him. By way of both Christianity and Mandaeism, he influenced Islam. By way of the baptizing group known as the Elchasaites, John's influence shaped Mani, whose religion was embraced by Saint Augustine before his conversion to Christianity. Manichaeism, as it is called, spread throughout central Asia all the way to China and persisted there until the modern era. Also by way of the Silk Road, and the presence of Mandaeans in Mesopotamia and Persia, John's immersion practice may have had an impact on religion in the Indian subcontinent. Today immersion rituals are widely practiced there, yet that seems to be an innovation from long after John's time, and there are plausible ways that groups ultimately influenced by John could have brought such practices to India. By all these means, the ripples of John's ritual and his teaching continue to spread today.

The conclusion of the book briefly reflects on how John's impact could be so widespread and yet in each instance, someone or something other than John became the focus of attention. John's talk of one who was to come explains how the one whom Jesus acclaimed as the greatest human being to ever live became the Christmaker, the forerunner of Jesus. There is thus a certain fittingness to John having receded into the background. Yet if we are to understand the people and traditions he influenced both directly and indirectly, it is necessary and appropriate that we bring him back into the center of our attention and give him a closer look.

Few have attempted to do what this book does, namely, offer a full-fledged biography of John the Baptist. Indeed, some have said it cannot be done.[3] Most books about John are historical surveys of the few details we know, or focus on how he is depicted in later art and storytelling. By the end of the next chapter, if you aren't already, I hope you will be persuaded that this is indeed possible. We have more information available than is widely known, and more of it is of historical value than is generally recognized. Yet it is not primarily from late and obscure sources that we derive our most important and valuable information about John. While most focus on John's testimony about Jesus, this book will take a closer look than others have at Jesus's testimony about John.

The Gospels show us the extent of John's influence on Jesus. The Gospel of Matthew summarizes the message of both in exactly the same way: repent, for the kingdom of God is at hand (3:2; 4:17). Matthew also indicates a shared palette of images, from the tree that fails to produce good fruit and is in danger of being cut down, to turns of phrase like "brood of vipers" and talk of a coming "Son of Man." Even though it is a given that ancient students provide an important window on their teachers, this has not been applied in depth or detail to the case of John and Jesus. Without Plato, we would know far less about Socrates than we do. Yet while there are still Platonists in our time, there are no Socratists. It is a common occurrence in history for a teacher to be eclipsed by their student. Yet even as in some ways that obscures the earlier figure from view, in other ways it allows us to bring them into sharper focus. The student provides a lens through which we are now forced to view their mentor, and lenses inevitably distort. Yet as someone who wears glasses, as well as being fascinated by astronomy, I know how powerful the positive potential of the lens is to bring what is distant and blurry into sharper focus.

Whether your primary aim is to get to know Jesus better, or to get to know John better, this book will make the case that we simply cannot do one without

---

3. For example, Knut Backhaus, "Echoes from the Wilderness: The Historical John the Baptist," in *Handbook for the Study of the Historical Jesus*, ed. Tom Holmén and Stanley E. Porter (Leiden: Brill, 2011), 2:1780, writes, "a biography of John the Baptist will never be written."

the other. John was a figure of unparalleled influence, and it is unsurprising that so many myths and legends emerged about him, and that his legacy has been and continues to be contested. This book brings John into sharper focus. As who he was and what he did becomes clearer, you'll come to know the voice crying in the wilderness, the new Elijah, the Baptist, the Christmaker, as you never have before.

A Rebellious Son

History is full of rebels, and they come in all shapes and sizes. Some rebel against parental authority and pursue their own dreams and desires. Some rebel against social norms and chart their own course in opposition to the status quo. Some rebel against a king or ruler, or against their religious heritage. Yet if history abounds in rebels, relatively few are rebels in all of these ways simultaneously. John the Baptist was one of those rare individuals. John's father was a priest, yet John did not follow in his father's footsteps even though the status of priest was a hereditary one that automatically passed from fathers to sons. More than that, John undermined the stability and the centrality of the temple and the priesthood by publicly offering an alternative means of forgiveness to the temple's sacrifices.[1] John spoke out against Herod Antipas, who ruled Galilee and Transjordan. He had negative things to say about other religious movements in his time, such as the Pharisees and Sadducees (Matt. 3:7; John 1:24). The few things that we know with relative certainty about John grab our attention. He is a fascinating individual, and we want to know more, to understand him better.

What leads someone to rebel in all these diverse ways? What sets a man against his father and his father's profession? Modern readers of biographies

---

1. On this as the meaning of a baptism for forgiveness of sins, see (among others) James D. G. Dunn, "Jesus and Purity: An Ongoing Debate," *New Testament Studies* 48 (2002): 459, https://doi.org/10.1017/S0028688502000279; Simon J. Joseph, *Jesus, Q, and the Dead Sea Scrolls: A Judaic Approach to Q* (Tübingen: Mohr Siebeck, 2012), 144–45. Had John been promoting a purity baptism, he would neither have been challenged about whether he had the authority to do so nor nicknamed the Baptist.

expect explanations that delve back into the individual's childhood, their family story and upbringing. Ancient historians and biographers were rarely interested in such details. Their failure to tell us what we want to know can be frustrating. Occasionally, however, despite their lack of interest in the psychology and motivations of the people they write about, ancient authors nevertheless provide enough details that historians can deduce the answers to our questions. This proves to be true in the case of John. Consider what we are told about John and his parents. Both the Gospel of Luke in the New Testament and the Mandaean Book of John record that John's father, Zechariah, was a priest. A Jewish priest in that era was above all else someone whose lineage traced back to Aaron, the brother of Moses, and who was thus permitted to offer sacrifice in the temple.

Most readers of this book will have no experience at all with the practice of animal sacrifice. Indeed, many may never have witnessed an animal being slaughtered at all. The practice of worship as most today think of it involves either quiet prayer and meditation or boisterous singing, not blood and the death of animals. Yet for ancient people, sacrifice was not merely a part of worship; it was the mode of expressing oneself to a deity par excellence. If you sinned and wanted to seek forgiveness, you offered sacrifice. If you experienced good fortune and were grateful, you offered sacrifice. It was central to religious life, and religion was woven throughout all aspects of a society. In Judaism in this era, most agreed that sacrifice could be legitimately offered in only one place: the temple in Jerusalem. That meant that just as sacrifice was central to worship, the temple and the city were the hub around which Jewish religious practice and identity revolved.

The New Testament tells us that John proclaimed a baptism for the forgiveness of sins. That means he was explicitly offering people what sacrifice offered but was offering it by another means, one that (unlike sacrifice) did not come with any other cost attached to it than sincere repentance and immersion in water. This is why we have characterized John as a radical, a rebel against not only his father's profession but his people's religious practice. In the next chapter, we will focus on how John came up with the idea that water could provide what the slaughter of animals and ritual manipulation of blood did. In this chapter, our aim is to dig back earlier. What set John on the path that would lead him to develop and proclaim a distinctive means of obtaining forgiveness for sins?

The manner in which someone goes against the expectations and demands of family or society can clue us in to things about their background and upbringing even when we lack sources that explicitly inform us about such matters. The son of a conservative pastor may rebel by joining a rock band. But in another scenario, the son of such a preacher might start another church in their town that competes with his father's. Both are rebels but of very different sorts, and the family story that led to each would be different. In the first instance, we would surmise that the rebellion was prompted by a strict upbringing that the son bristled against, most likely in adolescence. The religious values of the father are being cast aside. In the second case, the situation is very different. The son is rebelling precisely by pursuing his father's path and vocation but in a very different way from his father. We would have to listen to the sermons of both in order to figure out whether the son subscribed to the father's outlook but saw hypocrisy in his life and so set out to draw people elsewhere, or whether the son had a very different understanding of what the religion he was brought up in ought to be.

While we don't have anything akin to a sermon from John's father, Zechariah, we know enough about what John taught, and what one would have heard from a typical priest in that era, to be able to compare the two. John's teaching was not at odds with the values of his own tradition as far as ethics were concerned, although he called people to live up to them fully and even radically. We will dig into John's teaching in greater detail in a later chapter. For the moment, the key thing to note is that John was much more like the latter sort of figure we just described than the former. He was not rejecting his father's religion; he was promoting a different means of forgiveness while calling people to worship the same one God and to live righteously with a greater level of seriousness and devotion than he saw exemplified in their lives.

If you are thinking that you would love to know what happened in the family of Zechariah and Elizabeth, John's parents, that might have led John not to follow in his father's footsteps, to actively undermine the centrality of the institution his father served, then I have good news for you. As it happens, we have the clues we need to answer this question, and they have been right under our noses in the New Testament all along, albeit in a place that historians would consider unpromising. I am referring to the stories of John's parents and John's early years found in the Gospel of Luke.

Longing for a Son

The childhood of heroes is often shrouded in legends. This is true even in the case of figures much closer to our time than John the Baptist. For American readers, a useful comparison may be the story that is told, with no basis in history, that George Washington chopped down a cherry tree but then confessed when confronted. For British readers, it may be more useful to mention that (contrary to what you'll find repeated in many places on the internet) Winston Churchill was not born in a ladies' room at a dance. Down the ages, people have invented stories to fill in what they wished they knew. They have imagined what must have been the case for someone to have become the exceptional adult who made such an impact on history. It is understandable that this is how things happen. George Washington's parents did not foresee that he would be president of a new country, and Winston Churchill's did not know he would become a famous prime minister. Had either set of parents known the future, they might have made a greater effort to record more about their child's early years. By the time someone becomes famous and the world longs to know more of their story, the details and memories of their childhood have been mostly or entirely lost.

In ancient infancy stories, one tends to encounter few verifiable details. Instead they abound with miraculous signs and angelic visitations that presage who the child will become. All of this makes such materials seem unpromising to the historian. Yet that does not mean they can be dismissed outright as useless. Even when people concocted legends and stories that were more symbolic than literal description, they often included things they knew, setting their tales of wonders against the backdrop of places, people, and events about which they had actual information. The infancy stories about John are no different. We have already drawn on them in describing John as the son of a priest, a piece of information that fits well with what we know of John as an adult.[2] There are other crucial details in these stories as well.

The stories about Zechariah and Elizabeth in Luke 1 are very similar in style and themes to the stories about Hannah and the wife of Manoah in the Jewish

---

2. Knut Backhaus, "Echoes from the Wilderness: The Historical John the Baptist," in *Handbook for the Study of the Historical Jesus*, ed. Tom Holmén and Stanley E. Porter (Leiden: Brill, 2011), 2:1781–82.

Scriptures (1 Sam. 1–2; Judg. 13). Both of those women were without children and longed to have a son. In the patriarchal cultures of the ancient Mediterranean world, the main if not the only reason for marriage was to produce a male heir who could care for his parents when they became old and inherit whatever they left behind. The stories about Hannah and the wife of Manoah continue by narrating how, after God answered their prayers and granted them sons (Samuel and Samson, respectively), each dedicated her child to God. That dedication took an unusual form. Both Samson and Samuel were to be lifelong Nazirites (Judg. 13:5; 1 Sam. 1:11). Not to be confused with "Nazarenes," which means people from Nazareth, Nazirites were persons who made a vow and dedicated themselves to God for a particular period, such as until they had completed a task or fulfilled a promise (Num. 6). During the time of their vow, they refrained from cutting their hair and from all grape products. When the period of their vow was completed, they would shave their heads and go back to life as usual. Samson and Samuel, on the other hand, were dedicated from before they were born and were to remain Nazirites throughout their entire lives.

Scholars have noted the similarities with details in the infancy stories in the Gospel of Luke. Luke (or a source that he used) certainly drew on those scriptural narratives in crafting stories about John's childhood: the appearance of an angel to foretell the birth of the long-hoped-for child; poetic outbursts of praise from the mother and others. John is also said to refrain from wine and other fermented drinks (Luke 1:15), just as Samson and Samuel did. While John's hair is not mentioned, complete abstinence from fermented drinks is itself sufficient to indicate that John was being depicted like these other heroes of his people from long before him.

Historians, noting that Luke could have simply borrowed these details from famous stories, tend to dismiss their historical value. Yet we should not do so too hastily. There is a reason why stories about mothers who were categorized as barren remained popular down the ages. In a patriarchal culture in which a wife's chief duty was to provide a son for her husband, women who were themselves or whose husbands were infertile read those stories and hoped that God might do for them what God had done for others. The Gospel of Luke explicitly mentions that Zechariah prayed for a son (Luke 1:13). It is inconceivable that Elizabeth did not do likewise, especially in that ancient patriarchal context in which women shouldered all the blame for infertility. Elizabeth would have grown up hearing the many stories in Scripture about

Hannah and many other women to whom God had granted children after initially being unable to conceive. We can easily envisage her praying to God for a son and promising to dedicate him to God if God answered her prayer, just as Hannah had (1 Sam. 1:11). Then as now, one way that people respond to stories in Scripture is to pray, "God, please do for me what you did for them. When you do, I will do for you what they did."

If Elizabeth prayed such a prayer and made such a promise, it would explain how John's life unfolded thereafter and answer many of the questions we have been posing. Nazirites and priests were both dedicated to God by maintaining a higher level of ritual purity than others and following rules and restrictions that others didn't have to. While on duty, priests had to abstain from alcohol just as Nazirites did for the duration of their vow. Yet there is also an important difference between priests and Nazirites. While the Nazirites expressed their dedication to God by not cutting their hair, priests were required to keep their hair trimmed (Lev. 10:6; 21:10; cf. Ezek. 44:20). The Babylonian Talmud makes it explicit: what Nazirites were required to do priests were prohibited from doing. If Elizabeth made a vow to dedicate her child to God in the same manner as Hannah and the wife of Manoah had, then you can see the dilemma. If she bore a son, as the wife of a priest, that son would not merely be expected to become a priest; he would be a priest, because the role and status were hereditary. If she committed the boy to being a Nazirite, she put him in the situation of being required to simultaneously observe commands that contradicted one another. He had to refrain from trimming his hair and he had to trim his hair.

Before he was even capable of making choices, John was placed in the impossible situation of having to choose between the way of life inherited from his father and the way of life to which his mother had dedicated him. This experience set the stage for John to recognize that the torah, the Jewish law, did not answer every question and could impose contradictory demands. It was not only between the demands of being a priest and being a Nazirite that John found himself caught, pulled in two directions. One of the Ten Commandments requires children to honor their father and mother. What if your father wants you to follow in his footsteps as the law requires and to be a priest, while your mother has made a vow that you will be a Nazirite and wants you to keep it even though that prevents you from being a priest? The insight John gained from this situation that was forced upon him, that there were situations in which there was simply no way to do what the law required, would have a powerful influence on John's teaching and values, as we will explore in more detail later in this book.

Thus, while there is a great deal we wish we knew about Zechariah, Elizabeth, and their son, we can connect the dots and bring more of the story into sharper focus than has been done in the past. Elizabeth's vow can explain why, when we encounter John in his adult years, we find that he did not follow in his father's footsteps to become a priest. Zechariah presumably not only longed for a son but expected that if he ever had one, the boy would follow in his footsteps and be a priest. Zechariah would have been less than thrilled to learn that his wife had made a vow regarding the child, which prevented him from doing so. The torah (Num. 30) allows a husband to annul his wife's vow so long as he does so on the day that he learns of it. Why didn't he do so? The simplest answer is probably that it would have taken him more than a day to become aware of the incompatibility of being a Nazirite while being a priest. In all the discussions of these laws and of the life of John the Baptist that I read while working on this book, no one mentioned this. I'm guessing that it is also true for you who are reading this. It took a very specific set of circumstances for this to come up in the way it did for John.

There are other options as well. According to Luke, at that time, Zechariah became mute and unable to speak! It is interesting that the Jerusalem Talmud would later record a rabbinic discussion about precisely this question: What happens when a husband learns of a vow that his wife made and wishes to annul it but at the time is paralyzed and cannot speak (Nedarim 10:8:2)? Such a ruling might or might not have already been made in Zechariah's time. Indeed, for all we know, it may have been the case of Zechariah that led to the debate and to this ruling. The Gospel of Luke depicts Zechariah as being struck mute immediately after learning that he would have a son who was committed to the life of a Nazirite. There is no need to invoke a miracle in a way that historians cannot legitimately do in order to make sense of this. On a human level, we can understand how the news, however he heard it, would have impacted Zechariah. To long for a son, only to be told that he can never be a priest, would be a shock. It was a sufficiently traumatic experience for him to have been so shocked as to have temporarily lost the ability to speak. That in turn would have deprived him of the opportunity to annul his wife's vow.

But as we said, if this seems too far-fetched, to give too much credence to the details of an infancy story that probably has only a smattering of history woven through it, there is a simpler option. It is conceivable that Zechariah had not pondered the contradiction regarding the hair of priests and Nazirites. Let's be honest—most people have never noticed this, including those who read the Bible often. As something that simply had never come up in the lifetime of Zechariah and those he spoke with that first day after learning of his wife's vow, Zechariah likely didn't realize the implications of Elizabeth's vow until it was too late for him to annul it. Whatever the precise circumstances, at some point, he would have become aware of this. From then on, the tension in the household would have been palpable. The choice not to give John his father's name may reflect an awareness that John would not serve in the priesthood as his male ancestors had.

This reconstruction of John's backstory, while explored here in connection with the infancy traditions about him, is ultimately about things that were publicly visible and that would have been common knowledge about John. His hair, together with his abstinence from alcohol, would have made it clear to everyone who had significant contact with him that he at least *appeared* to be a Nazirite. That he was the son of a priest would also have been clear, as was his preaching and his baptism, which took aim at the temple's exclusive offer of a means of atonement. It is possible that the source Luke drew on wove a fanciful tale in an effort to make sense of these details and that we have now relied too heavily on it in our own reconstruction of John's life. Yet that is unavoidable, to some extent, with any ancient figure about whom we have these kinds of stories. What is most important is that the core elements of the ancient story, and thus of this one, are things that people saw and knew about John. Those are the things historians seek, on which to build a reconstruction of someone's life and in particular their early years. Our sources provide what we need, if only we take the time to dig into the sources, become aware of the ramifications of the information we have been provided, and connect the dots.

A Long-Haired Runaway at a Commune?

There are aspects of John's story that sound so familiar that we must be careful not to allow a mental image to form that is too modern or informed by recent history in ways that distort it. John's long hair did not have the same connotations as long hair did in the 1960s in the era of the hippie movement. For one thing, being a Nazirite was about dedication to service in the religion of one's ancestors according to the torah. It was anything but countercultural. In John's specific case, however, the tension between John's status as Nazirite and his status as priest would have pushed him in a countercultural direction, as he discovered that simply by virtue of ancestry and parental choice, he was put in an impossible situation. As the son of a priest, John would have had a higher level of education growing up than his average contemporary. Even without that background, he would have searched the Scriptures to make sense of his unique situation, torn between two sets of laws, each of which called him to a life of dedication to God and yet each of which was incompatible with the other. Sooner or later, he would have begun to notice some of those awkward details in the Scriptures that, for modern scholars, provide clues about the development of ancient Israel's religion. Samuel was not of priestly descent. He was a Nazirite. And *he offered sacrifices* (1 Sam. 7:9–10; 16:2–5). Yet John was being told that he would never be allowed to offer sacrifices even though he had the same status as the famous Samuel, as well as being the son of a priest. Far from being barred from offering sacrifices, one could make the case that he was doubly eligible to do so! Samuel offered those sacrifices in a variety of places, and yet in John's time, the view was that Jewish sacrifice must be offered only in the Jerusalem temple. John would have come to view the temple and its priesthood as having created a monopoly on the provision of forgiveness, one that disadvantaged those who lived far from it, those who struggled to afford an animal to offer, and many others—as well as excluding individuals like him from participating in the services the temple and its priesthood provided.

In light of what we were able to piece together about John's family, we know the choice that he faced. Zechariah, his father, would likely have confronted the long-haired John directly as he reached the age at which he could begin to participate in priestly duties.[3] John had not made a vow; his mother had. Zech-

---

3. Num. 4:3, 23, 30 and 8:23–24 in the Bible differ on the age at which Levites (presumably including priests) began to serve in the temple, either thirty or twenty-five. The Talmud, on the other hand, attributes to different rabbis views ranging from puberty to age twenty (b. Hullin 24b). The fact that John appears in public when, based on the information Luke provides, he was roughly in the age range the Bible indicates is likely significant. Whether the matter between John and his father came to a head much earlier or only when John approached that age is impossible to say. On the date of the fifteenth year of Tiberius Caesar's reign, which depending on how it is interpreted may mean anywhere from around

ariah may have demanded that he honor his father as the law commanded, cut his hair, renounce his mother's vow, and become a priest like his father before him. Yet doing that would break the very commandment he was being told to obey, because it would dishonor his mother. It would have been a no-win situation, with John disobeying the commandment to "honor your father *and* mother" no matter what he did. No matter what choice he made, he would be considered a rebellious son. If Zechariah demanded that John reject his mother's commitment made on his behalf before he was even born, John likely resented this. Ultimately he chose his mother's vow over his father's lineage.

When John chose his mother's vow over his father's vocation, it made him unable to serve as a priest. It may have angered Zechariah and John both. It is hard to imagine that they did not quarrel. It is entirely possible that Zechariah told his son when he came of age that if he would not cut his hair and follow in his father's footsteps, then he was no longer welcome in his house. It is also possible that John left to try to figure things out. Either way, Luke tells us that between his youth and the time when he appeared in public as a prophet, he was in the wilderness (Luke 1:80). Many have jumped to the conclusion that this means the Judean desert, but that is far from certain. Matthew 3:1 locates John's preaching there, but Luke 3:3 has John preaching in all the region in the vicinity of the Jordan River. The term translated "wilderness" in these and other texts about John does not specify a "desert" in the sense that English word has today. It is the word from which our English words "hermit" and "hermitage" are derived. If you visit the Monastery of Saint John in the Desert, built to provide a place of pilgrimage associated with John's time in the wilderness, you will find it to be anything but a desert. The hillsides are lush with vegetation. You will, however, need to take a winding road to get there. It is not in an arid location, and thus a desert in the modern sense, but it is relatively isolated. John left the place where he grew up—we'll return to the question

---

AD 25 to AD 29, see John P. Meier, *A Marginal Jew: Rethinking the Historical Jesus*, vol. 1, *The Roots of the Problem and the Person* (New Haven: Yale University Press, 1991), 374–75; Robert H. Stein, *Jesus the Messiah: A Survey of the Life of Christ* (Downers Grove, IL: InterVarsity Press, 2009), 57; I. Howard Marshall, *The Gospel of Luke*, New International Commentary on the New Testament (Grand Rapids: Eerdmans, 1978), 133. The information in John 2:20 places Jesus's temple action in the year AD 28, and that in turn suggests that John's public activity must have begun by around 27, if not earlier. That assumes, of course, that this information is correct, which it is impossible to determine with a high level of certainty.

of what town or village that might have been later in this chapter—and lived away from more heavily populated areas. We do not have historical evidence for precisely where John did this, but one location actually in the Judean desert has been proposed.

When I first visited the Monastery of Saint John in the Desert, I had a hard time finding it. You can see where it is on the map on your phone, yet it isn't immediately clear how to reach it. I was glad to have encountered this difficulty, because it led me to the most perfect place to ask for directions: the Essene Farm in Even Sapir. Despite the name, this center for healthy living and ecological wellness has nothing to do with the ancient group known as the Essenes. Yet I was still delighted because, as some readers will already know, it has been suggested that John the Baptist might have spent time among the Essenes or even been part of that group for a time. What better than to be able to honestly say that when I was looking for Saint John in the Desert, I stopped to ask for directions at the Essene Farm?

The site of Qumran, near the caves where the Dead Sea Scrolls were discovered, was an important site for the ancient Essenes, although not all of them lived in that community in the Judean desert. Essenes were found throughout the land, and if John had contact with them, it could have happened anywhere. The truth is that there are a few striking similarities and points of agreement between John and the Essenes and yet even sharper differences. That does not justify jumping to the conclusion that John spent time as an Essene, any more than points of agreement between Jesus and the Pharisees means that he actually belonged to that group for a time. In spite of this, it has become common to posit that John spent time at Qumran before eventually breaking with the group.

When one visits Qumran today, one is treated to a movie depicting the community's life. In it, one of the members of the community gets word about the death of someone named John and asks whether it might be the same John that used to be part of their community. The historical evidence doesn't justify treating this as though it were an established fact in this way. Let us imagine, however, that John did indeed leave home and head into the Judean desert. The site of Qumran provided relative isolation for the Essenes who lived there, concerned as they were with observing ritual purity rules with a greater strictness than most of their contemporaries. Yet we must not imagine them as completely cut off from contact with other people, any more than we should imagine John going into the wilderness and spending years or even months with no encounters with anyone else. Not only is the harsh environment of that region one that requires human cooperation for survival, but the cultural values that John and the Essenes shared emphasized community and hospitality. Even when we are not told in New Testament stories that other people were present than those explicitly mentioned, it is usually a safe assumption.

Regardless of whether John ever visited the site of Qumran, if he spent time even for a while somewhere in the vicinity, contact would have been made. Discovering that the son of a priest who knew and could read the Scriptures was nearby, they likely would have shared some of their foodstuff and engaged in conversation. Given the differences between John's outlook and their own, there would have been vigorous debates.

What has led scholars to think that John was influenced by the Essenes' ideas and practices? They understood their community of the faithful to be a temple, one that had access to alternatives to animal sacrifice when the temple could not provide what was needed. John's message also incorporates such ideas. They practiced immersion in water not just occasionally but daily. They had their headquarters in the wilderness of Judea, although their membership was found far and wide. They emphasized community and the sharing of wealth in common to promote equality. Their writings quote Isaiah 40:3, the famous text about a voice crying in the wilderness that the Gospels apply to John. In light of such points of contact, it is no wonder that people have suggested that John may even have been an Essene at some point in his life. Once John had been set at odds with his father, this may have opened him to other influences and perspectives that further cemented his stance and what he did. For example, John may have encountered Essene criticisms of the way things were done in the temple and felt they were kindred spirits. Because Essenes were found throughout the land and not only at Qumran, there is no need to speculate that John may have become part of the Qumran community. John may have known Essenes even before he left home. Indeed, if John knew any Essenes, they might have recommended to him that he join their group and pointed him to Qumran as a place to seek not only a new place to live but answers to his questions.

Nevertheless, there are enough differences between John and the Essenes that it makes more sense to view him as a conversation partner with them rather than an adherent. In the ancient world, as today, people adopted ideas from other traditions without in any sense converting to them. John also developed ideas and practices that have no parallels in the Dead Sea Scrolls. Some of the points of similarity are also relatively superficial. John and the Essenes may have criticized the priesthood, but nothing indicates that they did so for the same reasons. John did not embrace any of the specific teachings or emphases of the Essenes, as far as we can tell, nor did he find a ready-made concept of atonement through water in the practices of the Essenes—or of any other group, for that matter. The Essenes were eager to resume worshiping in the temple, and to the extent that they considered prayers and immersions to substitute for sacrifice, it was a temporary measure. John, as we will see in the chapters that follow in more detail, was actually challenging the centrality and necessity of the temple altogether.

We must also consider that an outsider looking at groups in a different culture, and a historian looking back at a different era, will perceive a lot of similarities among groups in any society. It is difficult to determine when we are dealing with direct borrowing and when it is a case of shared heritage. John's overall outlook and approach was different not only from that of the Essenes but from that of all his contemporaries more generally. Other groups before John's time practiced immersions for purity. That was not what John offered in his baptism for the forgiveness of sins. No other group proclaimed a new means of forgiveness to crowds while warning them that the kingdom of God was about to dawn. No other group that we know of deliberately sought to attract rather than exclude those whom the pious looked down upon as sinners. No other group threatened the temple as directly as we will see that John did. No other group emphasized economic justice quite so centrally in their ethical teaching. Setting John in his context is important for understanding what he shared with his contemporaries, which was plenty. Against that backdrop, we also see all the more clearly what his innovations were, what his contributions were to the history of religion.

If the Essenes took pioneering steps in the direction of developing (or becoming) an alternative to the temple, John went much further in two ways that are closely connected. He threw open wide the gates of access to a means of atonement that, if the Essenes developed it at all, they kept for themselves and used as a temporary measure until such time as the Jerusalem priests offered sacrifice and observed purity in the way the Essenes considered necessary. John, we shall see, saw the physical temple as no longer necessary, for it had never truly been necessary. True, sacrifice could be a means of seeking forgiveness, but John found that the Scriptures themselves never claimed that such offerings were the *only* way to obtain forgiveness. Because of claims about its exclusive mediation of access to atonement and to the presence of God, the temple became an idol, a stationary physical representation of the divine presence that sought to lock in God's forgiveness and favor in one place, in the midst of one tribe. Where the Essenes continued to focus on the temple even as they took steps in the direction of developing an alternative, John looked back to the tabernacle that could provide access to the divine presence throughout the land, and forward to Ezekiel's vision of a new temple that would gush forth healing waters. We will explore how John brought these ideas and emphases together in the next chapter.

LOCUSTS AND WILD HONEY

It was not only because John left home that he would have had reason for concern about where his next meal would come from. For John, this was a situation that had no long-term prospect of being resolved. Since John would never serve as a priest in the manner stipulated in the Scriptures, John would also never be eligible to share in the food that was provided to priests. The Scriptures told how the tribe of Levi from which priests came had not been given an inheritance of land like the other tribes (Deut. 10:9; 18:1–8; Josh. 13:14, 33; 18:7; Ezek. 44:28). Instead they were to serve the Lord and the people as facilitators of worship and to live from the tithes and offerings collected by the temple. Once he left home, unless he found a different job, he would not have a way of obtaining food. If he sought to maintain priestly purity nonetheless, then the involvement of other people in providing him with food would be a problem, as none of them (with the possible exception of Essenes) would observe the rules that he needed to. This combination of factors can explain why John became famous for eating locusts and wild honey (Mark 1:6). These seem like a strange combination to modern ears and unfortunately have contributed to the idea of John as something of a raving wild man who ate bugs. Nothing could be further from the truth. Locusts and grasshoppers were kosher, that is, food that was acceptable to eat according to Jewish law. These two foods had two things in common: they were available at no cost if someone could find them, and no other person was involved in providing them. For an individual who was without other income and concerned to remain ritually pure, these two items presented themselves as obvious choices.

As John wandered in the wilderness, his mind would have turned to the Israelites wandering in the wilderness, the stories of which are told in the Torah as well as being the focus of some of the Psalms. The temptations they faced there and the choices they made would shape their later history, right down to John's own time. By the time he left there, he would have a vision for calling his contemporaries to revisit the wilderness generation's experience and to make a choice different from the one they made, to obey God rather than disobey. Whether he was ever tempted to doubt God's provision, by the time he taught his disciples how to pray, it included an emphasis on not worrying about the next day and trusting God for daily sustenance. Interestingly, scientists can tell us what the manna was that the Israelites ate in the wilderness. A similar word is still used in Arabic for either the hardened sap of the tamarisk tree, or even more frequently, the secretion of insects that feed on that sap and leave behind a sweet edible remainder from the process. The tamarisk is one of the few trees that can grow close to the Dead Sea's salty terrain. It is striking that John ate insects and honey, while manna was apparently a product of insects that tasted like honey. Perhaps John's "honey" was none other than the manna of the Israelites. Honey made from sap and from the secretion of insects that feed on sap is still called "manna honey" in some places even today.

Although at this point in our exploration of John's life we are still some way from him attracting followers, hearing what Jesus and others had to say about him is crucial even at this stage for getting a sense of the impression he made on his contemporaries, what was distinctive about his eating habits, and much else. Those later activities and characteristics clue us in further about John's formative years.

Birds of a Feather

Rebels tend to attract other rebels around them; and those who become part of the entourage of a rebel will be perceived as rebels themselves. It should come as no surprise to discover that John's most famous follower, Jesus of Nazareth, was accused of being a rebellious son as well. While we have had to deduce aspects of John's relationship with his parents by reading between the lines of our sources, Jesus explicitly says that he was so accused (refer-ring to himself indirectly, as he apparently often did, using the Aramaic idiom "Son of Man," which meant "a human being" or "someone"). When he talked about this accusation, Jesus mentioned John right alongside himself; indeed, he began with John. The Gospels of Matthew and Luke each record a version of this saying of Jesus:

> "John came neither eating nor drinking, and they say, 'He has a demon'; the Son of Man came eating and drinking, and they say, 'Look, a glutton and a drunkard, a friend of tax collectors and sinners!' Yet wisdom is vindicated by her deeds." (Matt. 11:18–19)

> "John the Baptist has come eating no bread and drinking no wine, and you say, 'He has a demon'; the Son of Man has come eating and drink-ing, and you say, 'Look, a glutton and a drunkard, a friend of tax collec-tors and sinners!' Nevertheless, wisdom is vindicated by all her children." (Luke 7:33–34)

That there were differences between John and Jesus is undoubtedly true. The point of the saying, however, is not what distinguished them. The point is rather that, despite any perceived differences, they were the targets of related criticisms. What people were saying about Jesus was that he deserved to be stoned to death for being a rebellious son! Deuteronomy 21:18–21 says,

> If someone has a stubborn and rebellious son who will not obey his father and mother, who does not heed them when they discipline him, then his father and his mother shall take hold of him and bring him out to the elders of his town at the gate of that place. They shall say to the elders of his town, "This son of ours is stubborn and rebellious. He will not obey us. He is a glutton and a drunkard." Then all the men of the town shall stone him to death. So you shall purge the evil from your midst; and all Israel will hear, and be afraid.

When people referred to Jesus being "a glutton and a drunkard," they were using the precise wording of the law in Deuteronomy. Rabbinic tradition has preserved ample evidence that this law was not enforced and that most people if not all agreed that it should not be. Mishnah Sanhedrin 8:4 specifies that if one parent has died, the law cannot be applied since it specifically mentions both parents. If Joseph had died by the time of Jesus's public activity, Jesus was off the hook—not that we have reason to believe that Mary thought of Jesus as a rebel against her authority, much less one who ought to be executed for that reason. Nonetheless, people could say that Jesus *deserved* to be punished as a rebellious son even if his mother supported him and even if the law could not and would not be applied. The Gospels record Jesus explicitly mentioning such accusations and connecting them with John as well.

What made Jesus a rebellious son in the eyes of his contemporaries? Perhaps it was simply the fact that as eldest son, he did not remain at home to care for his mother and siblings by leading the family business. Perhaps it was because he grew up in a household that supported the priesthood and temple and now had joined a group with a vision diametrically opposed to that. A priest's eldest or only son who refused to become a priest himself and instead set out to undermine the work of the priesthood would naturally be accused of being a rebel, out of his mind, even under the influence of a demon. Jesus, too, was accused of having a demon (Mark 3:22; John 10:20), which makes clear that the point of what Jesus said was not how he and John were different.

It isn't clear what it meant to say that John "came neither eating nor drinking." Luke's addition of "bread" and "wine" shows his awareness of a problem with the statement. The saying cannot be literally true. If it were, John would have starved to death. Perhaps John observed a stringent level of purity, avoiding food handled by anyone else, in an effort to ensure that his rite would be an acceptable offering to God. Temple offerings required stringent purity, and so he may have reasoned that his baptism must follow the same rules or even more stringent ones. Perhaps his reliance on food provided by God was an act of faith that John felt symbolized what it meant to obey, in contrast with the ancestors of the wilderness generation who had grumbled about the manna and the quails God provided (Exod. 16). Jesus also emphasized relying on what God provided. At the same time, he was also known for his habit of dining with mixed groups that transgressed social divides. Did John ever get invited to meals, and if so, did he accept the invitation? We simply do not know. Jesus was a key person in the movement John had begun, and whatever differences there may have been between them, people made the same kinds of accusations about them both nonetheless. *That* was the point.

The Heavenly Father

Biographers in the past have sometimes surmised that Jesus's emphasis on God as Father might have been a response to his father dying when he was young. The heavenly Father substituted for the absent earthly father. Given what we have explored here, there is reason to think that this sort of insight would more naturally have occurred to John than to Jesus. His mission set him at odds with his father and probably emerged within a context of already-existing tensions within the family. Like Jesus after him, John was criticized for not being "about his father's business." Of course, by the time John began his activity, Zechariah might have died. Whether Zechariah lived long enough to criticize John for what he was doing we cannot know, but as in the case of Jesus, so too in John's case, we need have no doubt that others in the community voiced criticisms on Zechariah's behalf. John may have faced actual criticism from his father while he was alive or imagined disapproval after he died, or both. On the other hand, it could be that John's criticism of the temple was based on Zechariah's own frustrations that he expressed at home and that John grew up hearing. If so, and if it was John rather than Jesus who first referred to the temple as "my father's house," the double meaning for John would in this case add extra poignancy. When people have engaged in this sort of psychologizing in the past with respect to Jesus, it has usually seemed like a stretch. In John's case, it seems much less so. Indeed, it seems to fit rather perfectly.

The Mandaean Book of John narrates Zechariah's distress over John's birth even as his fellow priests articulate that John's birth is bad news for the temple (18:55–59; 27:5–8). John, on the other hand, says at one point in the same work that he stands in his father's strength and praises him (19:1–16). It is clear in the context that John is not referring to Zechariah. In that same passage, he also emphasizes that he built no house in Judea and that he has not loved "the intellect that drank wine" or "physical sustenance." That John's relationship to his celestial rather than terrestrial father comes up in a context that also mentions his eating and drinking habits, the same themes that converge in the Gospels, is surely no coincidence. Both reflect the impact of things John said and did. In Luke's version of Jesus's saying about himself and John as rebellious sons, Jesus concludes his rejoinder to the criticism by saying, "Wisdom is justified by her children." Both John and Jesus not only had a heavenly father but were

Wisdom's children as well. Jesus would later refer to God's Wisdom sending prophets whom the people killed (Luke 11:49). He had John particularly in mind on that occasion as well, as we shall see in a later chapter when we explore his statement about the blood of all the prophets from Abel to Zechariah.

In Luke 11:1, it is in response to a request that Jesus teaches his disciples the famous prayer known as the Lord's Prayer or Our Father. The request is that he teach them to pray *as John taught his disciples to pray*. This request is made to Jesus as one who had himself been a disciple of John. While it does not necessarily mean that they wanted him to repeat a prayer heard from John, or that the precise wording of the Lord's Prayer originates with John, we have very good reason to view it as, at the very least, echoing John's teaching and emphases. What we know of John's emphases corresponds to the prayer's key points: God as Father, the arrival of the kingdom of God, provision of food in manna-like fashion, and forgiveness. The wilderness wanderings of the Israelites form the background to the prayer, and this, too, corresponds to the setting of John's activity even better than it does to that of Jesus. They worried about food for the coming day. They faced testing and also tested God. They gave in to temptation and failed to do God's will. Israel is described as God's firstborn son (Exod. 4:22–23) who is called to worship God their Father in the wilderness (Exod. 3:18). The story of Israel's time in the wilderness is a thread that runs throughout the prayer.[4] The wilderness served as the symbolic backdrop for John's thought and teaching, even at those times when it was not his literal geographic setting.

This is not to say that the prayer in the form we now have it originally stems from John the Baptist. That is a possibility but not what I am claiming here. What I do think we can say with confidence is that the key ideas in the prayer were not Jesus's innovation but reflect John's influence on him. Jesus inherited this outlook from John, and it became part and parcel of his teaching as well. Jesus spoke a great deal about "this generation." In John's view, their generation was called to revisit the situation of the wilderness generation and decide for themselves whether they would repeat the mistakes of the past or instead make

4. I am indebted here to Jeffrey Gibson's book *The Disciples' Prayer: The Prayer Jesus Taught in Its Historical Setting* (Minneapolis: Fortress, 2015), for highlighting the way that the prayer has the wilderness generation as its background and framework.

different choices. The prayer is a plea to God for help in doing the latter rather than the former. John did not go into the wilderness to get away from people or to start a community that sought isolation from the wider society. He focused his activity there because he was calling people to revisit the wilderness as a prelude to becoming the people that Israel had been called to be from its beginnings. Past generations had failed to live up to that calling. John proclaimed that the time had arrived when God would offer one final opportunity to his people. The choice was whether to be a tree that would bear fruit or a tree that would be cut down (Matt. 3:8–10).

Those themes were all taken up by Jesus in his own activity, because he viewed his own mission as a continuation of what John had begun (Matt. 7:18–20; 12:33; 21:43). He taught his disciples to pray, if not a prayer that John had taught him, at the very least a prayer that was woven through with the themes and emphases of John's own mission and teaching. They were to differentiate themselves from the wilderness generation and needed to pray for God's help to be faithful in doing so. John spoke of God as his Father and considered himself to be "about his father's business," as Jesus also came to. That business was to call the people to renewal by way of the wilderness, to step into the vocation of being not merely God's firstborn son but God's *obedient* son who honors the Father as the Father deserves.

When the early Christians told the story of Jesus being tempted in the wilderness as recorded in Matthew 4:1–11 and Luke 4:1–14, they depicted him facing the temptations that the people of Israel had faced in the wilderness. Jesus is then depicted as responding in precisely the manner the book of Deuteronomy said the Israelites ought to have. In view of what we have discussed thus far, it becomes clear that the gospel authors were not merely interested in depicting Jesus as one who recapitulates the story of Israel, or as one who obeys God, but more specifically as one who lives out that which John the Baptist called for. We shall return later to the question of whether John viewed Jesus as his successor. For now, the point is to show how the references to the wilderness in connection with John should be understood, and how what the Gospels say about Jesus and the wilderness also helps us fill in the picture of John. When we trace the threads that run through the gospel stories about Jesus, the prayer taught by Jesus, and the parables and imagery Jesus himself used, we find they converge not only in the wilderness but in *John* in the wilderness.

In the Spirit and Power of Elijah

Through his clothing and perhaps in other ways, John styled himself after Elijah, and the similarities were perceived by others. Noting John's choice to identify with this prophetic precursor helps us to avoid misinterpreting what it meant for John to spend time in the wilderness. Elijah was apparently from somewhere in the region in Transjordan where John was active. He directly confronted kings and priests. Elijah fled to the wilderness at one point because he had the impression that he had failed, but even then not because he desired to become a hermit. Instead, he went back to Horeb, Mount Sinai, the place where in a real sense it all began (1 Kings 19). There he found strength and divine reassurance in order that he might be better prepared to engage with political and religious powers when he returned. His response to his renewed commissioning and the encouragement he received was to make a disciple, Elisha. In the same way, John's movement in the wilderness was not about withdrawal but preparation by going back to beginnings. Those who recognized the similarity between him and Elijah saw him as not a monk seeking solitude but a divine spokesperson ready to shake things up even more than he had thus far. By styling himself as Elijah, John may also have been seeking to convey that he considered the leaders of his time no better than the Baal-worshiping Ahab and Jezebel. It may also be that both John and Elijah long before him each found inspiration in the still earlier story of Moses's encounter with God in the wilderness (Exod. 3).

In Luke 1:80, we are told that John, like Elijah, was in the wilderness not as the locus of his public activity but as a prelude to it. Luke 3:2–3 then goes on to say that "the word of God came to John son of Zechariah in the wilderness." This portrays him as a prophet standing in the long line of those who had been sent to God's people with a message. Luke further specifies that John's public activity was carried out in all the region around the Jordan. This included places in Transjordan that were at the very least close to locations that feature in the story of Elijah, and perhaps where Elijah was originally from. Regardless of whether John went to Jerusalem himself, he certainly sent emissaries there. In the next chapter, we will look at one famous instance when John did so, in a story you quite likely already know. Like Jesus after him, John would have returned to deserted places to pray and seek renewed strength. The aim was always to return ready to continue calling his contemporaries to change their ways and prepare for the arrival of God's kingdom.

JOHN AS PRIEST AND KING?

The temple in Jerusalem had been built by Solomon, the ruling king. It had been renovated by Herod, another king. For John to have challenged the legitimacy of the temple, it required him to have not only prophetic but royal authority. When we ask whether anyone in John's time thought of him as a royal as well as a priestly figure, it brings us back to stories about John's childhood, not only in the Gospel of Luke but also in another early Christian source from the second century known as the Infancy Gospel (or Protevangelium) of James. In Luke's Gospel, Zechariah's response to the announcement of his son's birth is to say that the God of Israel has "raised up a horn of salvation for us in the house of his servant David" (Luke 1:69). The Infancy Gospel of James, after Herod's order to slaughter male infants in Bethlehem, suddenly introduces Elizabeth fleeing with John to protect him from Herod. The reader gets the distinct impression that its author was incorporating already-existing material at this point. Here is a brief excerpt (from the translation by M. R. James):

> But Elizabeth, when she heard that they were looking for John, took him and went up into the hill-country seeking a place where she could hide him, but there was no hiding-place to be found. Elizabeth groaned and said with a loud voice, "O mountain of God, receive a mother with a child." For Elizabeth was not able to climb it. The mountain immediately split in two and took her in. A light was continuously shining for them and an angel of the Lord was with them keeping watch over them.
>
> Now Herod sought for John and sent officers to Zechariah. They asked him, "Where have you hidden your son?" He answered them, "I am a priest of God and am continually in the temple of the Lord. I don't know where my son is." The officers left and informed Herod, who was angered and said, "His son is to be king over Israel."

The very presence of this material in the Infancy Gospel of James is surprising, given the way it interrupts the story about Jesus that is being told. The details are equally surprising, and yet they converge with things that readers do not always notice in the New Testament. In the Infancy Gospel of James, Herod says that John the Baptist will become king! It is unlikely that a Christian author would invent the idea that John was a royal figure; this material probably comes from followers of John the Baptist. Since it is unlikely that any of John's followers would have come up with the idea that he was to rule Israel after he was executed, the claim that John was in some way a kingly figure must have originated during John's lifetime. It is extremely difficult to imagine it being invented later.

John's movement may have viewed him as a priest-king of a more legitimate sort than the Hasmonean rulers had been. The Hasmonean dynasty was the one that ruled prior to Herod, and they claimed the titles of both high priest and king. Given his activity at the springs near Salim or Salem (John 3:23), perhaps John applied to himself the idea that the author of the letter to the Hebrews would later apply to Jesus, that of a priest-king "after the order of Melchizedek" (Heb. 7:17, quoting Ps. 110:4). Melchizedek was king of Salem, and while that city was later identified with Jerusalem, it more likely originally denoted a place actually called Salem. That is one of the places in the vicinity of which John baptized. Perhaps he did so precisely because of the connection with Melchizedek. John challenged the temple as one with royal, priestly, and prophetic authority to do so. Yet John is remembered as having predicted that someone even greater and more powerful than he would soon be along. We will discuss what John is likely to have meant by that prediction, and how it relates to the idea of John himself as king, in a later chapter.

For the present, let us simply note that the Infancy Gospel of James provides an answer, at least implicitly, to a question we had not yet asked concerning John's childhood. Where was he born? The Gospel of Luke says only that Elizabeth resided in a "town of Judah" in the hill country (Luke 1:39). Which one, and why doesn't Luke give its name? Churches marking the supposed sites of John's birth and Mary's visit to Elizabeth would eventually be built in Ein Kerem, a village that today has been incorporated into the city of Jerusalem. The Infancy Gospel of James, however, by depicting Elizabeth and John as fleeing the massacre that Herod ordered, points to another possibility, namely, Bethlehem. It is possible that John's heritage as someone who was of priestly descent and also from Bethlehem led some to think that he himself might embody both roles, whether through actual connections with royal as well as priestly lines in his ancestry, or through the mere symbolism of place and association.

CONCLUSION

After reading the introduction to this book, some may have felt that I was being too optimistic about our ability to bring John into clearer focus. After all, there is so much we don't know. When it comes to the focus of the present chapter, however, not only have important details about John hopefully become clear, but some of those details are precisely the sorts of things that we wish we knew about Jesus of Nazareth and other ancient individuals yet do not. Modern readers of biographies are interested in psychology. We want to know who the biggest influences on a person were. Relationship with parents is a particularly important detail. Ancient biographers were largely uninterested in such matters and do not tend to provide the information we are looking for. This creates a disconnect between modern readers and ancient texts. In the case of John, the situation is different. We get a sense not only of what he did that led to him being held in high esteem by many and yet feared and opposed by others but also what led him to do what he did—the motives, influences, and aims.

Perhaps the most surprising discovery is what was hinted at in the text all along, namely, the division between father and son, between Zechariah and John. We have found within our sources a plausible explanation for why John did not follow in his footsteps, why he left home, and even why Zechariah might have had some sort of seizure that left him temporarily unable to speak on learning about who his son was destined to be. The Mandaean sources add additional details about John's return from the wilderness to which he had fled for safety. In their version of the story, it is a being from the celestial realm that whisks John away, rather than his mother Elizabeth (who plays this role in the Infancy Gospel of James). When John returns from his time away, the Mandaean Book of John (so called because of its focus on John the Baptist) tells how Elizabeth spotted John, recognized him, and ran out to kiss him, neglecting even to veil herself before doing so. That source also says that Zechariah decided to divorce Elizabeth because of this. Whether there is any historical reminiscence in such details, they reflect a memory of something that the Gospel of Luke and other Christian sources also hint at. The division between John and his father was connected with a division between his father and mother. The Gospel of Luke provides the evidence that allows us to deduce Elizabeth's prayer and vow and the conundrum it presented for John as well as his parents. All of this was there already in our sources, waiting to be noticed. Yet no one has put together the pieces of this puzzle until now, most likely because those who had studied these sources have rarely been interested in John as a figure in his own right.

Having clarified these starting points, we may now move on to an exploration in detail of the innovation that made John famous: baptism for the forgiveness of sins. John did not merely reject the path of becoming a priest himself. He started a movement that, if it caught on completely, could undermine and bring to an end the activity of the temple altogether. John's baptism constitutes a remarkable innovation. But where did John get the idea for his ritual from? How did he come up with it? What Scriptures did he appeal to? The chapter that follows tells that story.

In the next chapter, we'll trace the sources of John's idea that living water (the Aramaic idiom for flowing water) could play a role in the forgiveness of sins. Later in the book, we will explore ways that John expected his baptism to accomplish even more than that. Baptism was intended to be a means not merely to find forgiveness but to achieve a deeper spiritual renewal, a rebirth of the individual and of the people of Israel as a whole. This, too, may have been not merely a potential consequence of the baptism he innovated but one of the reasons that he developed it in the first place. Sacrifices had been offered for centuries, indeed millennia, yet the people continued to fail to live differently. John hoped that his baptism would offer people not merely a different means of obtaining the same forgiveness but a canceling of humanity's debt to God in a spiritual year of Jubilee, which would free the people from sin as they underwent a new exodus. They were to pass through the waters, determined this time to live into the calling of the Israelites to be a kingdom of priests, a chosen people that brings honor to God's name rather than causes it to be profaned (see Ezek. 36:23, which is probably echoed in the Lord's Prayer when it asks God to hallow or sanctify the divine name). It was time for the new covenant that God would write on his people's hearts (Jer. 31:31–34).

I Will Destroy This Temple

S ometimes visiting a specific place provides a new angle on the topic you are researching and writing about. During the trip to the Holy Land that I mentioned earlier in the book, focused on visiting sites connected with John the Baptist, I saw a number of such places. One that was particularly helpful was an unexpected one, although with hindsight perhaps it should have been obvious that it was just the right location to provide insights into John the Baptist. Although I was already a few days into the trip, I still hadn't yet found time for sustained writing, just the jotting down of quick notes. When I did finally find time to sit and write at length for the first time during that trip, it was by a swimming pool. People I was traveling with went swimming, while I sat to write. It immediately became clear that I was at a perfect place to think about John the Baptist and how his baptism related to other kinds of immersion that people engaged in.

One of the things it is easy to miss about John the Baptist is the significance of his nickname, considered against the backdrop of his time and place. In the century or two before John lived, the immersion pool (what in Judaism is called a *mikveh*) had gone from being rare to being commonplace. While the torah requires washing in numerous contexts, it does not specifically require immersion of one's entire body. Leviticus 15 mentions several circumstances in which washing one's entire body was required, but even then it does not specify that this be accomplished through immersion. There are other ways that one can wash their whole body. More often than not, something on a smaller scale, such as washing of hands and feet, is all that is specified (as in Exod. 30:17–21, for example). Nevertheless, for whatever reason, immersion pools and the practice of immersing oneself completely caught on and spread, so that in John's time, one could find them everywhere. Greek and Roman bathing had also spread and become popular. In other words, people were immersing themselves in water more often than at any point in the history of the Jewish people.

Hence the puzzle: In an era when nearly everyone was immersing, how does someone become known as "John the Immerser"?

Nicknames function by distinguishing people from others. An Englishman in New York may be nicknamed Sting the Englishman (not that Sting needs another nickname). It is difficult to imagine a circumstance, on the other hand, in which he would get nicknamed "the Englishman" while living in his native England. There he is just another Englishman in a country full of them. This tells us something crucially important about John the Baptist. He was not merely someone who liked bathing, nor was he merely an advocate for the ritual purity washings that his contemporaries were accustomed to practicing. His baptism was something else, something capable of earning him a nickname.

The Gospels tell us what set it apart. The immersion John practiced and proclaimed was not a bath for cleanliness or an ablution to remove ritual defilement but a baptism of repentance for the forgiveness of sins (Mark 1:4). Impurity and sin were occasionally connected, and the former might be used as a symbol of the latter, but ultimately they are very different things.[1] Contact with a corpse rendered you ritually defiled, but it was not a sin. Indeed, in some circumstances, it was essential to touch a corpse in order *not* to sin—for example, in the case of a son burying his father in the family tomb and thus honoring his father, or when someone happened across a corpse and was the only person who could intervene to ensure burial before sundown as the law required (Num. 19:11–13; Deut. 21:23; Tob. 1:17). A woman who gave birth was impure for a time, but in no sense was childbirth considered sinful. Washing was required to deal with the impurity, but since the action that made one impure was not sinful, the washing was in no sense thought of as removing sin.

---

1. Jürgen K. Zangenberg, "Pure Stone: Archaeological Evidence for Jewish Purity Practices in Late Second Temple Judaism (Miqwa'ot and Stone Vessels)," in *Purity and the Forming of Religious Traditions in the Ancient Mediterranean World and Ancient Judaism*, ed. Christian Frevel and Christophe Nihan, Dynamics in the History of Religions 3 (Leiden: Brill, 2013), 540–41, https://doi.org/10.1163/9789004232297_020.

In short, John became universally known as the Baptist (or if you prefer, since the Greek word was not yet a technical term, we might as easily call him the Immerser, the Dipper, or the Dunker). This happened in an era when people immersed regularly for the purpose of purity or pleasure. That tells us something incredibly important about John. He was saying and doing things that stood out even within that context. His baptism was understood to be distinctive in that context as well. In theory, calling someone "the Baptist" could indicate that he was a member in a movement of Baptists (just as nowadays this terminology denotes membership in a particular type of Protestant church). However, the fact that we have so many references to "John's baptism" indicates that John was an innovator, an inventor, rather than a follower. The rite that was associated with him was attributed to him personally and not an already-existing group to which he belonged. Christian baptism has become so familiar that it could easily not even occur to someone today to ask how John came up with the idea that one could immerse to express repentance and obtain forgiveness for one's sins. The universal assumption in the ancient world was that, if one needed to seek forgiveness for having offended a deity, or for that matter if one wanted to express gratitude to a deity, animal sacrifice was the way to accomplish this.

The slaughter of animals was the focus of the worship that took place in the temple in Jerusalem. Indeed, it was the focus of the worship of any gods, anywhere in the Roman world. Today, in contrast, few English speakers have ever witnessed an animal sacrifice. The word "worship" does not bring to mind the sounds of animals and the sight of blood. (If you don't believe me, bring a bull into any church, lead it up to the altar at the front, and proceed to slit its throat. I guarantee that those present will not applaud you as having made a positive contribution to their worship service.)

How did we end up with such drastically different assumptions and practices from our ancient forebears? It is thanks in large part to John the Baptist.[2] While John was definitely not the first person to recommend immersing in wa-

<hr>

2. To be sure, the Christian view of Jesus's death as the only sacrifice necessary plays a role in the widespread shift. It is unlikely, on the other hand, that this view would have emerged in this offshoot of John's movement had John not first led the way in promoting an alternative means of seeking atonement. Indeed, it may be that Christians connected baptism with Jesus's death viewed as a sacrifice precisely because many felt that baptism apart from sacrifice lacked something they considered crucial.

ter, as we have already seen, there is no clear evidence that anyone prior to John interpreted immersion in water as carrying the significance that he attributed to it. John was definitely the first to promote a baptism for the forgiveness of sins and call people far and wide to experience it.

The Marketplace of Forgiveness

Before we consider the *how* of John's development of baptism, we need to consider the *why*. What led him to seek out an alternative to temple sacrifice? In the previous chapter, we saw how John, as a priest by descent but a Nazirite by maternal vow, found himself unable to pursue his father's profession. With Scripture dictating what he could not do, John would have turned to those same Scriptures to explore what he could do, what he ought to do.

As the story of Hannah had inspired John's mother, the story of Hannah's son Samuel no doubt inspired John. According to 1 Samuel 1:1, Samuel was an Ephraimite. According to Jewish law, only the descendants of Aaron could be priests. Samuel was from the wrong tribe to be able to be a priest, yet according to the Scriptures, he nonetheless offered sacrifices (see 1 Sam. 7:9–10). Samuel, a Nazirite who was not a priest, did what the torah said only priests could do, and in the stories about him, there is no hint that it was controversial, much less illegal. (Even when the author of 1 Chronicles 6:22–35 turned Samuel into a Levite, which would have allowed him to serve in the temple in other capacities, that still would not have given him the right to be a priest and to offer sacrifices as priests alone were supposed to, as emphasized just a few verses later in 1 Chronicles 6:48–49.)

Samuel was not alone in this. Others, like Elijah, had also done likewise, and elsewhere than in Jerusalem (1 Kings 18:20–40). The same Scriptures that told of God choosing a place authorized for sacrifices and a priesthood descended from Aaron also showed that God had authorized others to act despite these constraints. It is surely no coincidence that Elijah and Samuel were both figures whose life and appearance John would emulate and with whom his contemporaries compared him.

As a result of his examination of the Scriptures in light of his own experience, John would have drawn a conclusion that to many today might seem radical, although it was likely far less so in his time. The torah was not perfect and unified. It was something good, but it was a human product, and the Jewish Scriptures themselves tell of times when the greatest heroes of the faith lived in ways that were at odds with its precepts. This was a key insight of John's that influenced Jesus, as we see from his willingness to view something that Moses legislated (divorce) as at odds with God's original intention (Mark 10:5–6). Whether John had any inkling of how scholars would account for this, namely, that the Torah in its present form did not exist and was not widely known until much later, is difficult to guess. Archaeological evidence shows that the widespread observance of the details of the laws in torah was a relatively recent phenomenon in John's time.[3] The Hasmonean rulers actively promoted it, and when they did so they undoubtedly framed their effort as a return to tradition rather than an innovation. Many in John's time, but by no means all, would have accepted that view of things. It doesn't necessarily even require a generation to pass for something new to become widely accepted as the way things have always been done. John recognized that things were more complex. We do not know whether he was influenced by those in his time who preserved a strong memory of the fact that torah was something relatively new in the history of Israel. As we will see in the next chapter, however, John's views and teaching on this subject resonated with a certain subset of his contemporaries who had sought to hang on to an older way of doing things that came to be proscribed in the torah itself.

As John explored and reflected further, he would have noticed a variety of additional points in the Scriptures that challenged the ultimacy of the temple in Jerusalem. Many of these are themes that eventually became part of the heritage of Christianity, as they inherited an emphasis on these Scriptures from John. For example, as Solomon dedicated the temple in Jerusalem, he was recorded to have emphasized that no such edifice could contain their God (1 Kings 8:24 // 2 Chron. 2:6). The story of Samuel conveyed that there had in fact been an earlier house of God of some sort, located at Shiloh (1 Sam. 1:24). Before that, there had been the tabernacle, which could move around from place to place. It was not difficult to see that the innovation of building a temple and restricting sacrifice to one site was at best an ambivalent development. It

---

3. On this, see especially Yonatan Adler, *The Origins of Judaism: An Archaeological-Historical Reappraisal* (New Haven: Yale University Press, 2022).

meant some people would have difficulty accessing forgiveness, residing many days' journey away, while others would be within easy walking distance.

Moreover, as the temple came to be thought of as the place where God's presence dwelt, Solomon's disclaimers notwithstanding, people came to think of the place and the city as sacrosanct, sure to be protected by God no matter what. Jeremiah 7:1–15 connects these threads, castigating the people for thinking they could do evil and then present themselves before God in the temple, relying on its presence in their midst as a safeguard. Jeremiah's accusation that they had made God's house a "den of robbers" would be echoed by Jesus in a famous incident we explore a little later in this chapter, and we have good reason to think that Jesus was not only echoing Jeremiah but doing so in a manner that he had learned from his mentor John. Jesus's own disciples would continue this theme, emphasizing that God does not dwell in temples or in statues, whether built by gentiles or Israelites (Acts 7:48; 17:24–28). Referring to both equally as "what human hands have made" conveyed that even the temple in Jerusalem was an idol.

What was John to do with respect to his own predicament in light of this information from Scripture? In theory, John could have taken the route of offering sacrifices elsewhere than in Jerusalem. Doing so would have been even more controversial than what he did, and far fewer would have embraced his message and his practice. He would simply have been viewed by most people as a violator of torah, rather than a prophet of the God revealed in those texts. I don't think it was only concern about controversy that led John not to pursue that option, however. As he considered the inequity of limiting sacrifice to a single place, he also noticed the inequity of requiring animal sacrifice at all. Some could scarcely afford to do so, while others could do so easily. The torah often provided a cheaper alternative for the poor, but that smaller offering still represented a hardship for many people, one greater than the cost of a bull to the most wealthy. Here, too, we see John's teaching carried on by Jesus, as he compared the offerings made by a poor widow to those made by the wealthy (Mark 12:41–44).

In addition to the cost of the sacrifice, it also took wealth to be able to travel from afar to the temple. The geographical location where one happened to have been born thus impacted people's access to forgiveness in much the same way different financial circumstances did. If he was going to chart an unconventional path, he might as well do something truly innovative, rather than merely emulate a bygone practice that few would be willing to accept. Thus John sought a way to separate forgiveness from monetary cost and to set it free to be experienced everywhere. John's concern for social and economic justice in the way he taught people to live (Luke 3:10–14) is woven into the very fabric of his baptism itself. These are themes that we also find on the lips of Jesus in the Gospels, and we can deduce that they are a result of John's influence on Jesus.

Streams of Living Water

If the above explains why John sought a way to carry out a priestly role that was independent of the temple and did not require animal sacrifice, the question remains why he developed this particular rite as the means to accomplishing that. One doesn't have to look very far in the Jewish Scriptures before one encounters texts that might, given John's background and perspective, have inspired him and provided him with what he was looking for. John sought a way to carry out a priestly role without actually serving as a priest in the temple.

One text that seems likely to have influenced John is the very beginning of Isaiah. We know that language from later in the book, about preparing the way of the Lord, was central to his self-understanding (Isa. 40:3; see Mark 1:3; John 1:23). Isaiah 1:10–15 addresses the people of Judah as Sodom and Gomorrah and declares that God is fed up with their sacrifices. What does God want instead? The answer is provided in 1:16–18: "Wash yourselves; make yourselves clean; remove your evil deeds from before my eyes; cease to do evil; learn to do good; seek justice; rescue the oppressed; defend the orphan; plead for the widow." It is difficult to imagine a more perfect summary of what John emphasized, and so we should view this as a text that was important to John. Wash yourselves and do what is right, the very beginning of Isaiah said. The second part of the book of Isaiah comes from the time when Persia had replaced Babylonia as the empire in which the Jews who had been carried off into exile found themselves. It depicts a return of the exiles to their homeland via the wilderness.

Many in John's time viewed the exile as still ongoing, despite Jeremiah's prediction that it would last seventy years, and despite Daniel's revision of that to seventy weeks of years (i.e., 490 years). The dates envisaged by both predictions had come and gone in John's time. Something was wrong. Perhaps John, in his study of the Scriptures, perceived that the exiles had not made their return *spiritually* by way of the wilderness. The wilderness generation had famously grumbled and failed at the tests they faced, setting the stage for a history that was (according to Scripture) altogether lacking in fidelity to God and the justice that God demanded of the chosen people. John's message was not for people to withdraw from society to the desert, as the community at Qumran chose to, but rather to stand where their ancestors had stood in the wilderness and make a different choice. They were to undergo the passage through water just as their ancestors had. Their ancestors had proven unfaithful when tested. They had failed repeatedly, and God had judged them for it. John's own generation thus could not and must not rely on descent from illustrious ancestors as a basis for expecting God's favor.

John was not "a voice crying in the wilderness" but, as Isaiah said, a voice who called people to prepare the way of the Lord in the wilderness. There was wilderness throughout the region, and the Gospels make reference to John traveling about so that various such wilderness places could serve as the symbolic backdrop as he proclaimed his message.[4]

Others in John's time felt sure that, even if there had been a delay, God would soon act to liberate and exalt his chosen people. John's message was the opposite: judgment and condemnation were imminent, not salvation and blessing. The axe is at the root of the trees, John said (Matt. 3:10 // Luke 3:9). God views the people of Israel the way the owner of fruit trees views trees that have failed to produce good fruit for many years. They have been given a chance long enough. The time has come to cut them down. There is a short time remaining in which it might just be possible to turn things around, but it will take a national movement of repentance and reform. That was John's aim.

Rabbi Abraham Joshua Heschel has argued that prophets are primarily not people who hear voices or see visions but people who *feel* intensely and are persuaded that God feels as they feel.[5] Like so many of the prophets of ancient

---

4. Daniel W. McManigal, *A Baptism of Judgment in the Fire of the Holy Spirit: John's Eschatological Proclamation in Matthew 3*, Library of New Testament Studies (London: Bloomsbury, 2019), 96–102, offers a concise overview of the symbolism of the wilderness in ancient Israel's prophets and then in the activity of John and Jesus.

5. Abraham J. Heschel, *The Prophets*, Perennial Classics (New York: HarperCollins, 2001), 31.

Israel, we see in John a strong emotional response to economic injustice and to people's attempt to salve their consciences with sacrifices. We see outrage at the complacency of believing that God is on our side because of who we are, regardless of what we do. The writings of those earlier prophets, not surprisingly, provided inspiration for John in their details and not just in general. But John did not just take up their message. As we can tell from the words he is remembered to have uttered, and the impact they had on people, John felt these things strongly. In his words and actions, his passion for justice and a radical reform of his society comes through loud and clear.

Another possible source of inspiration for John's baptism is the depiction of an ideal temple in the final chapter of the book of Ezekiel. Many interpreters understood it to be a temple that already existed in heaven, regardless of whether it would also become an earthly reality in the future. This beautiful and perfect temple was what people hoped for in the aftermath of the destruction of the temple by the Babylonians in or around 586 BC. What happened next left people disappointed. Once exiles who had been carried off by the Babylonians were able to return to Jerusalem and rebuild, the reality of the situation was that they were in no position financially to construct something that could live up to the grandeur of the temple the Babylonians had destroyed, never mind Ezekiel's vision of a superior one. Haggai 2:3 records some of the initial impressions: "Who is left among you who saw this house in its former glory? How does it look to you now? Is it not in your sight as nothing?" In other words, people had felt disappointed with the second temple right from the start. The disruption of the line of rightful priests and the desecration of the temple by the Syrian king Antiochus IV a couple of centuries later served to confirm the sense many had that the postexilic temple was not one that God took pleasure in or was interested in preserving.

Immediately before John's time, however, there had been a significant change. Herod the Great had funded extensive renovations and expansions, making the structure truly grandiose. But to whose honor? God's or Herod's? It still wasn't what Ezekiel had predicted. John may have been particularly struck by the way, in Ezekiel's account of his vision, a river of water issued forth from the altar and flowed out from there, exiting the temple and bringing the benefits of the atoning sacrifices offered within it to all the land (47:1–12). Earlier in the book, a future time had been promised when God would sprinkle the nation with water and cleanse them of their sins, giving a new heart so that the nation at long last becomes obedient (36:25–27). Some or all of this water imagery in Ezekiel, associated with forgiveness of sin as well as with addressing the deeper roots of sin, would also have provided John with sources of inspiration.

There is also the imagery of the exodus. The Israelites had passed through water to leave behind slavery and enter the promised land. On the way between the two, they faced the trial of the wilderness, which proved to be the downfall of that first generation. Yet the exodus was not the first time in the biblical narrative that there had been an effort to make a new start by means of water. The original creation had begun by separating the waters of the primordial deep (Gen. 1:7). However, the humans that dwelt in the original promised land, the garden of Eden, had also gone astray according to the story (Gen. 3:6–24). So too with Noah (Gen. 6–9), there had been a return of the primordial deep and a new creation. Then the exodus. Each of these crucial moments in God's interaction with humanity involved water and the making of a new covenant.

In addition to the way water brought judgment on humanity as a whole or on the Egyptians pursuing the Israelites, water also served to rescue and cleanse those who were being brought into a new era and a new existence. Water was used symbolically as well as featuring in the stories literally. Before receiving the covenant at Mount Sinai, the Israelites were commanded to wash their clothes and presumably themselves as well (Exod. 19:10–14). The institution of the Levitical priesthood also involved washing or bathing (Exod. 29:4). Each time a new order was brought into existence by God, it emerged through water. John may have been harnessing the resonances of not just each of these stories individually but the combination of them.

Literally passing through water was not the key, of course, as the stories and John's teaching about them made abundantly clear. Obedience was the crucial thing that was called for, and that time and time again throughout human history had been lacking. In each instance, there had been something like a new creation, and yet the people who entered it proved to be just like those in the world that perished. That was likely why John coupled his water rite with the imagery of the wilderness, to remind those who underwent his baptism that they could experience the exodus and yet fail to inherit the promised land. It was a different generation that crossed the Jordan, the river that John made a focus of his baptismal activity at least some of the time. According to tradition, the site where Jesus was baptized by John was the very site where the Israelites had crossed into the land, led by Joshua. It is impossible to know how far back that tradition goes, and so John might or might not have liked that particular site because of the added symbolism it provided.

Another possible background has been proposed for John's baptism. At some point, the custom was developed for those who convert to Judaism to undergo what is called proselyte baptism. If that practice existed before John's time, and gentiles who wanted to become part of the Jewish people underwent an immersion, then it might seem that that would have provided a poignant symbolism John could harness. By calling his fellow Jews to be baptized, John would have been saying that not only foreigners who become Jews but every Israelite needs to undergo their own conversion. It isn't enough to be a descendant of Abraham. The inhabitants of Idumea and Arabia were descendants of Abraham as well, yet the covenant was not with them. Nor was the covenant simply the possession of the descendants of Israel either. Anyone could join themselves to the covenant people, and John reasoned that anyone could remove themselves by choosing not to be faithful to the covenant and thus reject it. The symbolism of John calling his fellow Jews to convert to Judaism would be powerful, yet there is a hitch. In fact, there is more than one. First, we do not have any evidence of proselyte baptism before John's time. It is entirely possible that John's call to conversion inspired the practice of making gentiles who converted undergo immersion, rather than vice versa. Second, because gentiles had never before been immersed to deal with ritual impurity in the manner prescribed in torah, it is likely that the immersion associated with conversion was a purity immersion.[6] In other words, it did not represent a baptism of repentance for the forgiveness of sins. It was instead the first (and thus highly symbolic) purity immersion by a gentile who converted to Judaism. It would be the first of many, to be carried out in accordance with torah whenever they

6. T. F. Torrance, "Proselyte Baptism," *New Testament Studies* 1 (1954): 150–52, https://doi.org/10.1017/S0028688500003696, cites a footnote to the Soncino edition of the Talmud Bavli, b. Yevamot 48b, to the effect that the proselyte's previous sins were forgiven. The Talmud does not state that, and even if it did, that would not change the fact that the source dates from centuries after John's time. Torrance also cites the Mishnah, m. Pesahim 8, which in fact makes clear through its discussion not only of gentile converts but of mourners who have contracted corpse impurity that the discussion is about immersion for impurity. See also Knut Backhaus, "Echoes from the Wilderness: The Historical John the Baptist," in *Handbook for the Study of the Historical Jesus*, ed. Tom Holmén and Stanley E. Porter (Leiden: Brill, 2011), 2:1760.

contracted ritual impurity. Even if John was not advocating proselyte baptism for Israelites, however, John clearly did say that each person must make their own choice and not rely on having been born into a particular heritage. In doing so, John was not entirely unlike the Christian tradition that would much, much later bear his name: the Baptists.

Just as we must be cautious about interpreting John's baptism through the lens of later Jewish practices, we must likewise not assume that every aspect of later Christian baptismal practice tells us something about what John taught and did. In particular, many assume that John's baptism was, like Christian baptism, a onetime conversion experience. Yet there is good reason to think that John's baptism was something that one could undergo more than once. If baptism for forgiveness was a substitute for or alternative to sacrifice for forgiveness, then it would have made more sense for it to be something repeatable. That is in fact the Mandaean practice to this day. Among the Mandaeans, baptism is something done regularly at certain festivals and times of year, just like the sacrifices connected with major feasts in Judaism before the destruction of the temple. Mandaean baptism is also something that one can seek at any point one is aware of needing forgiveness.

When Christians turned baptism into a onetime identification with Jesus in his death and resurrection, problems immediately arose. This is the reason that multiple Christian texts in the first and second centuries wrestled with the problem of postbaptismal sin (Heb. 6:4–8; Shepherd of Hermas, Mandate 4.3.1–2).[7] Baptism was assumed to mediate forgiveness, and thus if you underwent it and could do it only once, you had to be very careful from then on. It is difficult for modern Christians, used to envisaging forgiveness as always available, to understand why the early Christians thought as they did. The answer is simple, once we understand that John's baptism was a repeatable rite for the forgiveness of sins. Turn that repeatable act into something that you can do only once, and suddenly you have a problem. This is why the emperor Constantine famously postponed being baptized until his deathbed. He was

---

7. See further Benjamin A. Edsall, *The Reception of Paul and Early Christian Initiation: History and Hermeneutics* (Cambridge: Cambridge University Press, 2019), 88; Joel Mokhoathi, "Christian Piety and Pardon: The Vindication of Post-baptismal Sins," *Pharos Journal of Theology* 99 (2018), http://www.pharosjot.com; David Brattston, "The Forgiveness of Post-baptismal Sin in Ancient Christianity," *Churchman* 105 (1991): 332–49.

not the only one to try to find a way to postpone their one opportunity to be forgiven, thereby avoiding finding themselves a baptized Christian who messed up and was now without hope.[8]

As we mentioned in the last chapter, many would chalk John's distinctive emphases up to a time they assume he spent at Qumran living with the Essenes. The basis for this is in fact little more than a few striking similarities, which are far outnumbered by the differences, some of which are quite stark. While both John and the Dead Sea Scrolls quoted Isaiah 40:3 in relation to their own identity and mission, that is in fact not an indication of anything other than shared Scriptures. If a Baptist pastor and an Anglican priest preach on the same text, it does not mean that one was originally a member of the other's denomination. The Essenes immersed with greater frequency than others, but it was in immersion pools, as was the common practice, and it was for the same reason—ritual purification. John's choice of rivers and other natural flowing water may have been a deliberate one in order to make unambiguous that the baptism he proclaimed was something else entirely. John's immersion rite was repeatable just as purity immersions were, but the significance was different.

Scholars have, for the most part, stopped drawing the conclusion that Jesus must have been a Pharisee, a Zealot, or a Stoic because of similarities between him and them. An outsider looking at differences between Christian denominations today might see clearly that the things the groups hold in common are far, far greater in number than the things that divide them. Those inside the groups, on the other hand, know how important those differences are to them. The differences between John and the Essenes are of precisely this sort. This is not to say that John might not have borrowed ideas from the Essenes, just as we can envisage Jesus being influenced by Hillel or the Pharisees in general (he subscribed to their view of the afterlife, after all), without it being necessary to posit that he was at some point a member of that group. While the Essenes were eagerly looking forward to returning to the temple to worship there, John shows no sign of sharing that desire. Indeed, a number of texts, and a famous public disturbance attributed to one of John's disciples, convey the opposite, that John's activity was a threat to the temple.

---

8. Eusebius, *Life of Constantine* 4.61–63.

Preaching That Rocks the Temple

The Mandaean Book of John depicts John's teaching as causing more than a little disturbance specifically focused on the temple.

> John, leave from our town! John, leave from our city!
> At your voice the house of the people quaked!
> At the sound of your teaching the temple quaked!
> At the sound of your refrains the dome of the priests quaked!
> (27:6–8, author's translation)

We could have deduced that John's baptism placed him at odds with the aims of the temple in Jerusalem even without Mandaean sources. The clearest indication of this comes from an action carried out by John's follower, Jesus of Nazareth, while still a part of John's movement. All four Gospels in the New Testament record that Jesus did something disruptive in the temple. You may have heard it called "the cleansing of the temple," but it isn't clear that the action was about purification. Without the sale of sacrificial animals, the temple could not function. The issue might have been the location where this was taking place, within Herod's newly built outer court, the Court of the Gentiles. As a new addition by Herod and not part of Solomon's Temple, it might have seemed legitimate to use that place to conduct business crucial to the operation of the temple, the sale of sacrificial animals, so that people who traveled from afar could purchase an animal somewhere conveniently located. Doing that in an area designated part of the temple, and one designated for worship by non-Israelites, nonetheless had ramifications. It is not impossible that Jesus might have wished to banish commerce (even if temple related) and animal dung from these precincts and might have proclaimed that God's house is "a house of prayer for all nations," which buying and selling turned into "a den of thieves" (Mark 11:17).

That is not, however, the only possible interpretation of his action. Stopping the sale of animals and exchange of currency could symbolize stopping the temple's activity altogether. Jesus is remembered as having spoken about the temple's destruction (Mark 13), and the Gospel of John connects Jesus's action in the temple courts with a saying about the temple being destroyed (John 2:19). That saying is a version of one that the other gospels try to distance from Jesus, which comes up at his trial. The evidence points to Jesus having in fact made some sort of a threat that he would destroy the temple and rebuild it, or build another, in three days (Mark 14:58; Matt. 26:61). On the gist of this, and how it was understood in the first instance, the Gospels agree.

My favorite way of referring to this action by Jesus is as the "temple tantrum." That, however, is because I love puns. Alas, this way of referring to the incident is also misleading. What Jesus did was not an instinctive outburst on the spur of the moment. It was a well-thought-out symbolic action. The Gospel of John depicts Jesus taking the time to make a whip out of cords to chase out the animals. The Gospel of Mark says that Jesus visited the temple and looked around, then returned the following day to cause his famous disturbance (Mark 11:11, 15–17). Mark also mentions that he did not let people use the outer courts of the temple as a shortcut through which they carried merchandise. The temple complex was a third of a mile wide, and I suspect that you might be willing to forgive those tired ancient people who, having walked in from the countryside, chose to take the shortest route possible to their destination even if it meant going through sacred space. Surely it was okay to sell animals and exchange currency in Herod's newly added Court of the Gentiles and to use it as a shortcut? Jesus's words in the various gospels highlight a number of interrelated facets of that space. Herod had taken it upon himself to reconfigure and expand the temple. It was a truly impressive structure, making Jerusalem a sight to behold. Did he have the right to do so? David and Solomon had needed special authorization to do what they did. Prophets like Elijah had offered sacrifice in other places, and presumably they, too, were authorized to do so.

John the prophet was now offering an alternative to sacrifice that didn't require people to come to this place that glorified Herod and national pride as much as the God who was supposed to be its very reason for existence. Yet the addition of the Court of the Gentiles pointed to the hope that Isaiah and other prophets had expressed, that the nations would be attracted to worship the God of Israel. Did the people respond to that with eschatological enthusiasm? No, according to the Gospels, the locals responded by using the place of worship allocated to non-Jews for their own convenience, selling sacrificial animals there and using it as a shortcut for the transportation of other goods. As far as John was concerned, the temple was not currently a place that was being used to honor God in the manner that God wished, nor was it being used to fulfill the predictions of the prophets. It is easy to understand why John viewed the temple as standing in the way of the people becoming truly righteous, rather than serving to accomplish that purpose.

So it was that John came to predict that God would destroy that temple and replace it. That message was delivered to the priests and others present in the temple by John's follower Jesus of Nazareth. Jesus's action in the temple and his words about the temple have received a great deal of attention over the years. What interpreters thus far have missed is that Jesus's words and action in the temple were a message from John the Baptist. The Gospel of John makes this clear in two ways.

First, it situates the incident at a time prior to Herod's imprisonment of John. Now, historians are often skeptical of the value of this information, since it disagrees with the earlier New Testament Gospels, which place the temple action at the very end, just before Jesus's arrest and execution. Generally, if multiple sources agree, that is strong evidence in favor of their collective testimony. This isn't a case of three against one, however, with Matthew, Mark, and Luke lined up in agreement against John. Matthew and Luke used Mark and follow the chronology of that gospel. As a result, it is rather a case of one against one, Mark versus John. Since Mark narrates only one visit of Jesus to Jerusalem, there was nowhere else that the temple incident could be included.

The second way John's Gospel makes it clear that it really does mean that Jesus did these things when still connected with John's movement is by providing the date. His challengers say that work on the temple had been going on for forty-six years (John 2:20). Herod's renovation project began in 20 BC, making this around AD 27.[9] While historians disagree about precisely when to date the marriage between Herod Antipas and Herodias, and then after that John's execution, none places these events in or before the year 27.

Thus when Jesus carried out his action in the temple, it would have been perceived as a message from John, who was still at large and leading his movement. Jesus was not acting alone or as leader of a group of his own. His ac-

---

9. On this, see James F. McGrath, "'Destroy This Temple': Issues of History in John 2:13–22," in *John, Jesus, and History*, ed. Paul N. Anderson, Felix Just, and Tom Thatcher (Atlanta: Society of Biblical Literature, 2009), 2:40, https://doi.org/10.2307/j.ctt16ptndz.8; Tamás Visi, "The Chronology of John the Baptist and the Crucifixion of Jesus of Nazareth," *Journal for the Study of the Historical Jesus* 18 (2020): 17, https://doi.org/10.1163/17455197-2019003.

tion would have been perceived as that of a follower of John the Baptist. This explains Jesus's response to those who challenged his authority to do things like this (Mark 11:28). He said he will tell them the source of his authority if they answer a question of his first (Mark 11:29–30): What is the source of and authority behind John's baptism? Thus Jesus himself explicitly connected his action in the temple, and his authority to do what he did, to John.

This connects directly with something that the Jewish historian Josephus tells us about John the Baptist. In his *Jewish Antiquities*, Josephus writes that Herod feared John's substantial influence with the people, which might make it possible for him to raise a rebellion. For that reason, he had him executed. One particular phrase is striking in connection with Jesus's action in the temple. Josephus says that people "seemed ready to do anything he [John] should advise" (*Jewish Antiquities* 18.118). We know of nothing that John's followers did that might have conveyed this impression to Herod Antipas, with a single exception: Jesus's action in the temple. That this incident might be what Josephus had in mind, and might have led quite rapidly to John's arrest and eventually his execution, helps us to understand the association of the event with Jesus's death in the Gospels. It was the execution of his mentor, more than anything else, that would have persuaded Jesus that he, too, might be destined for the same fate if he seeks to be John's successor or, more than that, the "one who is to come" that John predicted.

Interestingly, the Gospels attribute John's arrest to his criticism of Herod's marriage to his brother's ex-wife Herodias. Josephus, in turn, says that people viewed Herod Antipas's defeat by the Arabian king Aretas as payback for Herod's execution of John. It is easy to miss the connection, unless you know that Herod's first wife, whom he divorced in order to marry Herodias, was Aretas's daughter.[10] Herod's marriages were thus the reason for conflict and tensions in which the king had, in John's view, recklessly embroiled his people. Speaking against a king's marriages was a challenge to not only their own authority but that of any heirs they might have as well. Speaking against the temple built by one's father also challenged the authority of that dynasty. John's words were politically charged and not merely religious, the two being inseparable in the ancient world.

10. Ross S. Kraemer, "Implicating Herodias and Her Daughter in the Death of John the Baptizer: A (Christian) Theological Strategy?," *Journal of Biblical Literature* 125 (2006): 324–25, https://doi.org/10.2307/27638363; Visi, "Chronology of John the Baptist," 7–9.

What did John have in mind when he sent Jesus to deliver a message that threatened the temple? There is no evidence that John himself or his followers were planning to tear down the temple themselves, as though that were something feasible for John and his entourage to accomplish. Yet that is what the words naturally seemed to mean: "I will destroy this temple and in three days rebuild it." Anyone who wants to understand the saying and the reaction of Jesus's contemporaries to it should ponder it while standing at the Kotel, the Western Wall (sometimes called the "Wailing Wall") in Jerusalem. That famous site in the old city of Jerusalem is the only part of Herod's temple complex as it existed in John's time that is still standing. After decades of renovations and expansion by the Herodians, it was impressive in its size and beauty. This was not an edifice akin to a cathedral but one the size of multiple sporting arenas. The central and most holy part of the temple, where sacrifices were offered, was more comparable in size to a cathedral. That was just one part of the temple complex in John's time, if the most sacred and important part. If someone today were to stand outside the Pentagon and say that they would destroy it, they'd be arrested and searched for explosives. Someone saying the equivalent in the first century would more likely be mocked, because the technological tools that make such a threat feasible to carry out in the present day were not available. The huge stones that Jesus's disciples found so impressive were not something they could budge even if all of them worked together (Mark 13:1). Nonetheless, even if it was implausible that they could carry out their threat, the person making it might nonetheless have been arrested even in the first century. The high priest served at the pleasure of the Roman authorities and represented their will to the people as well as representing the people in their interaction with the Romans. To threaten the building that was the heart and soul of the priesthood was a threat to Roman as well as Jewish political authority, and in some ways to the heart of Judaism itself as many people understood it.

As the first chapter of the book of Isaiah makes clear, however, railing against animal sacrifice did not need to be understood as opposed to religious piety. Isaiah, John, and many others spoke in such ways in order to call people to faithfulness to God, and away from a reliance on sacrifice as a means of avoiding God's wrath against their wrongdoing.

In John's message that Jesus delivered, "I will destroy" could represent John (or Jesus, or both) speaking as a prophet, with the meaning being that it was God threatening to destroy the temple. Alternatively, John could have been speaking metaphorically. By offering forgiveness without ties to location and purchase of animals, John was providing something that would render the temple obsolete. If you lived in Galilee and could be forgiven by repenting and immersing in a river, would you spend money to travel to Jerusalem, purchase an animal, and sacrifice it? John's baptism did indeed have the power to destroy the temple in that sense, to undermine the rationale for its existence and bankrupt it. The authorities knew it. The new community of the righteous that John was assembling would, in turn, themselves become a new temple in the midst of which God could dwell, a temple "not made by human hands" (Mark 14:58; see also Acts 7:48; 17:24).

The Gospel of John tries to reinterpret the saying about the temple being destroyed and rebuilt as though it had been a prediction of Jesus's death and resurrection. In the process, the author of the gospel acknowledges that no one present at the time understood that to be Jesus's meaning (John 2:19–22). That was a later reinterpretation from the perspective of hindsight. Nevertheless, if Jesus's temple action led to John's arrest and execution, which in turn prompted Jesus to reflect on the possibility that his path must end in a similar way, it becomes unsurprising that the New Testament Gospels connect Jesus's temple action with his death in the manner that they do.

John and Jesus were not the only critics of the temple in that era. One reason why John has sometimes been viewed as an Essene is that the Dead Sea Scrolls spend a lot of time dedicated to criticizing the temple and its priesthood. Their members included descendants of Zadok, the authorized holders of the high priesthood according to the Scriptures. They had been ousted almost two centuries earlier and looked forward to the day when God would restore them to their rightful place. But the Essenes were scarcely the only ones who had complaints about the temple. While one could easily imagine John, as the son of a priest who was alienated from the temple, feeling a certain kinship to the Essenes, John's aim was to directly challenge and provide an alternative to the temple, while the Essenes wanted to be back in it and in charge. They aimed to keep out impurity and create a small faithful community prepared to inherit what God had in store for the faithful remnant. John's aim, on the other hand, was to transform the nation, and perhaps more than that. He may have begun with a desire to reach the lost sheep of Israel, but at some point, he realized that the seemingly righteous were often worse in some respects than those easily categorized as sinners. A "brood of vipers" he would call them, a phrase that Jesus echoed, just as he echoed many of John's other turns of phrase and emphases (Matt. 3:7; 12:34; 23:33).

As we have seen, the Jewish Scriptures were full of imagery related to water. Rather than focusing on any one passage, John offered a rite that resonated with a wide array of Scriptures and yet was not singularly focused on any one of them. He took something familiar—immersion in water—and made it special, giving it new significance. He called people to make public their commitment to doing what is right by an action that made their decision visible, and thus made them accountable to one another. While the language of a temple "not made with human hands" could have had in view the heavenly sanctuary in which God dwelt, it could also denote the community that made themselves holy as living stones, cleansed and purified not just of ritual defilement but of wrongdoing, so that God could dwell in their midst. John does not appear to have taken any steps to create an organization with a clearly defined structure, perhaps because he thought that there was no prospect of a longer term in which such things might be helpful. Judgment was coming, and either there would be widespread repentance and God's wrath would be averted, or God would cut down the unfruitful trees and do something new. Yet if creating an organization was not John's means to accomplishing what he hoped for, forging a sense of community was crucial. There is little room for sin other than in our interaction with one another, and in the same way, there is little prospect of moral reform and improvement without assistance and accountability. The new temple that would be built to replace the old one would be built out of people, with John serving as the tool in God's hand as God constructed it. This idea, coupled with the availability of baptism without costly animal sacrifice in select sacred spaces, represented a radical revolution in forgiveness. Geographic and priestly monopolies on the provision of forgiveness were being broken. When Jesus spoke of living water that undermined the relevance of the debates between Jews and Samaritans about whether to worship in Jerusalem or on Mount Gerizim (John 4:21), he was conveying part of the essence of John's teaching.

Jesus the Baptizer

John opened forgiveness to all, irrespective of their ability to pay or to travel. But what about those who were unable to immerse themselves in a river or other flowing water as John demanded? In several stories in the Gospels, Jesus heals people without baptism being explicitly mentioned. Consider the stories about Jesus healing paralyzed individuals in Mark 2:1–12 (paralleled in Matt. 9:1–8) and John 5:1–15. In the one in Mark and Matthew, Jesus is in Capernaum, which he has made his base of operations. That was not far from the Jordan River's entrance into Lake Tiberias, but in both stories, the man is paralyzed. There is no mention of taking him to immerse in the river, and in the version in Mark, it is clear that they are in a house into which the man has been lowered through the roof, and the whole story unfolds there. The question thus arises whether Jesus, John's follower, pronounced people's sins forgiven without baptism, and if so, whether this was his innovation or something that John approved of and perhaps even taught his followers.

It would be surprising if John, opposed as he was to the way the temple and sacrifice restricted access to atonement, were to have denied access to those with disabilities, or for that matter anyone without ready access to a flowing water source into which one could immerse. While there were many springs around the land, many of them emptied into a well or resulted in a relatively small trickle, not providing a means of full immersion. Could baptism be carried out in such places using such water? Although the Mandaeans would later blame Christians for using nonflowing water for baptism, that does not necessarily reflect the stance of John. One possibility is that Jesus innovated, that he built on John's foundational principles while applying them in a manner that John himself had not—not because John was opposed to doing what Jesus did but simply because it never came up prior to his arrest and execution. The Gospel of John tells us that Jesus baptized, even if it immediately tries to insist that he didn't do so (John 4:1–2). If Jesus had departed from John's practice of baptism for forgiveness of sins, we would expect this to be clarified. We should thus envisage Jesus sprinkling or pouring water on paralytics when he pronounced their sins forgiven. It may also be that the versions of the story in the Gospels of Mark and John are deliberate attempts to separate Jesus's authority to forgive from John's baptism, so that the authority rested exclusively and uniquely with Jesus. In Matthew's version of the story, Jesus has just stepped out of a boat, arriving in his "own town," which in this context was presumably not Nazareth but Capernaum by the lake, which he had made his base of operations (Matt. 4:13). It may be that Jesus's practice was more rigidly faithful to John's than that of some of his later followers. A baptism could have taken place in that location.

Sometime in the first century, the early Christian manual of practice known as the Didache would offer instructions on what should be the norm—immersion in cold flowing water—and what the options were if this type of water was not available.[11] Mandaean sources, on the other hand, condemn Christians for baptizing in nonflowing water and blame Jesus for departing from John's teaching on the subject. This may reflect disagreements from a later time, when baptism using stagnant water became the norm rather than exception in Christianity, as is the case today. The Mandaean tradition in turn radicalized in the other direction, requiring that baptism be carried out exclusively in living water. Mandaeism also insists that baptism be carried out by someone with a priestly status, not in the sense of Aaronic descent, as in Judaism, but in the sense of being a Mandaean who has been apprenticed by a priest and trained to carry out baptisms with the appropriate ritual.

The question of who had the authority to carry out baptisms also came up within Christianity. These later disagreements appear to have been projected back onto John and Jesus. In their own time, however, we find no indication either of requiring ordination to carry out baptisms or about the kind of water used. Indeed, the language used is sufficiently ambiguous that scholars are uncertain whether John's baptism was always baptism of one person by another or could be self-administered.

Despite these uncertainties, some things are clear. Initially, Jesus served as John's emissary, bringing his message and the forgiveness of sins to people who could not come to where John was. From John's perspective, it was their repentance and faith that mattered most. In exceptional cases where they could not get to water, it could be brought to them.[12] That exceptions could be made for those

11. Didache 7 says baptism should be "in living water. But if you have not living water, baptize into other water; and if you can not in cold, in warm. But if you have not either, pour out water thrice upon the head." Here I provide the translation in the public domain by M. B. Riddle, from *The Ante-Nicene Fathers*, ed. Alexander Roberts and James Donaldson (1885–1887; repr., Peabody, MA: Hendrickson, 1994). Revised and edited for New Advent by Kevin Knight (http://www.newadvent.org/fathers/0714.htm).

12. According to E. S. Drower, *The Mandaeans of Iraq and Iran: Their Cults, Customs, Magic Legends, and Folklore* (Piscataway, NJ: Gorgias, 2019), 179, https://doi.org/10.31826/9781463208073, the Mandaeans bring water from the river to someone who is close to death and immerse him or her in it three times. I have never seen this done myself and so cannot speak to the details of the practice, but it does illustrate that such uses of river

who faced hardships in being baptized was to be expected, especially when we consider that John's baptism was an alternative to sacrifice. Leviticus abounds in references to less costly animals and offerings of flour that could be substituted by those who could not afford the standard option. For the poor, of course, even these could present a hardship, especially when coupled with a need to travel to Jerusalem. This was, as we discussed earlier in the chapter, one of John's motives in developing his baptismal alternative. On the other hand, if there had been no cost and no ritual involved, people would not take the need to deal with sin and guilt seriously. (Indeed, some seem not to have done so even within the context of the sacrificial system, especially if the cost was not a hardship for them.)

There was surely significant development and elaboration between the ritual John performed and taught others to undergo and the more elaborate baptismal rituals of the Mandaeans in later times. (If you have never seen a Mandaean baptism, this is a good point at which to go on YouTube and do so.) Yet we can be reasonably certain that there was a ritual element to John's baptism. He did not merely dunk people in water without ceremony. As we have already noted, people were bathing more than ever before. John must have included ritual elements that set his baptism apart from other types of immersion.

The best way to get behind the later developments to what John himself did is by triangulating from things that Mandaean and Christian baptism share in common. These point to John having invoked God and perhaps other celestial witnesses, a triple immersion, anointing with oil, and quite possibly other features such as burning of incense.[13] That one could be forgiven simply

water brought elsewhere could reflect the practice of devout adherents of John's. Down the ages, Mandaeism as a whole has consistently insisted that baptism in living water is the only acceptable kind. Recent innovations such as the use of tap water in some diaspora communities does not reflect historic practice. Neither, however, can we assume that the practice of ordination of priests, elaborate ritual, and rigidly rejecting the making of exceptions with respect to the mode of baptism are things that go back to John himself.

13. Mandaean baptism is described in Jorunn J. Buckley, *The Mandaeans: Ancient Texts and Modern People* (New York: Oxford University Press, 2002), 81–86; Drower, *Mandaeans of Iraq and Iran*, 100–118. While Christian baptism was explicitly differentiated from John's baptism, it is also the case that within Mandaeism, the ritual as practiced today is associated with names other than John's, which is on one level an attempt to indicate that baptism is both older than John and of celestial rather than terrestrial origin. Nevertheless, it may also reflect awareness that others contributed to the formation of the details of the baptismal ritual in its present form. See further Jon Olav Ryen, "Baptism in Jordan—for Christians

by immersing in flowing water would have been difficult to believe. Recall how widespread immersion was in that era. It would have made no sense to treat forgiveness of sin as something that happened more or less automatically through immersion. There had to be some words and ceremony that charged this otherwise common action with a significance that merely taking a bath lacked. By including the burning of incense, John would have associated his baptism with the history of offerings mediated by a priest in the temple. Ancient people were all but universally convinced that the right combination of words and actions could be powerful in ways that people today might categorize as supernatural. The baptismal ritual would have been understood in terms not only of atonement but also of exorcism and sealing or consecration. John's baptism was a profoundly transformative experience for those who underwent it. They had profound spiritual experiences, found themselves healed of illnesses, and felt relieved of burdens.

People undoubtedly responded to John's proclamation of forgiveness of sins in precisely the way onlookers are said to have responded when Jesus did it (Matt. 9:1–8). "This is blasphemy! None but God alone can forgive sins." This is not, as some would have it, an indication of Jesus's divinity. Nor would the same objection to John's baptism imply that he was claiming to be something other than a human being. Matthew's version shows how Jesus's justification of his words and actions was understood: God had given this authority to human beings. Jesus's statement, that the Son of Man has authority on earth to forgive sins, used an Aramaic expression ("son of man") that meant "a human being" or simply "someone." The crowds, of course, already knew it to be true that human beings could facilitate forgiveness. Priests could reassure individuals that their sacrifices were acceptable to God and thus that their sins were forgiven. Jesus's use of the passive indicated that he was speaking about having one's sins forgiven by God. The issue for those who objected in the crowd was that John and his group were declaring sins forgiven apart from the temple and apart from sacrifice. It seemed blasphemous because they dared to

---

and Gnostics: Remarkable Similarities between Old Syrian Baptismal Liturgies and the Mandaean Masbuta," *Journal of Ancient Christianity/Zeitschrift für Antikes Christentum* 13 (2009): 282–315, https://doi.org/10.1515/ZAC.2009.20. Although John's clothing as described in the New Testament is not something Mandaean priests would wear, it is likely that the Mandaean priesthood adopted the wearing of white robes in emulation of the Jewish priesthood, a connection that John had through birth.

claim the right to do something that God had, in their view, authorized only priests to do. When the man turned out to have been healed of his paralysis, it was taken to be divine confirmation of God's authorization of John and his representatives to do this work.

There was a close connection between baptism and healing. This is indicated by not only the connection in the Gospels in which Jesus both heals individuals and pronounces their sins forgiven but also the later church's practice and the association of exorcism with baptism in both Christianity and Mandaeism. John himself was undoubtedly aware of the story of Elisha sending Naaman to immerse in the Jordan River seven times in order to be healed of a skin disease (2 Kings 5:1–14)—yet another text in Scripture that may have influenced and inspired John and provided a symbolic scriptural backdrop for what he was doing.

Conclusion

John's frustrated desire to fulfill his priestly role led him to interpret familiar texts in creative ways and to challenge an institution that stood at the heart of his people's identity and piety, yet from which many felt alienated or at least distant (whether literally, metaphorically, or both). The response that John's message and his proclamation of baptism received from people far and wide shows that it offered something people were longing for. In a later chapter, we will delve further into the hope John had that his ritual and words would generate not merely moral reform but spiritual renewal.

As we saw toward the beginning of this chapter, it seems likely that the book of Isaiah had a particularly powerful influence on John as he was contemplating his vocation. The first chapter sounds as though it could have been a manifesto for John's mission. Here are some excerpts, worth quoting at length (here in the NRSVUE translation), because doing so helps provide a sense of just how strong and how numerous were the resonances and links between the opening of the book of Isaiah and John's message:

> Woe, sinful nation,
>   people laden with iniquity,
> offspring who do evil,
>   children who act corruptly,

who have forsaken the LORD,
　　who have despised the Holy One of Israel. . . .

Hear the word of the LORD,
　　you rulers of Sodom!
Listen to the teaching of our God,
　　you people of Gomorrah!
What to me is the multitude of your sacrifices?
　　says the LORD;
I have had enough of burnt offerings of rams
　　and the fat of fed beasts;
I do not delight in the blood of bulls
　　or of lambs or of goats.

When you come to appear before me,
　　who asked this from your hand?
　　Trample my courts no more!
Bringing offerings is futile;
　　incense is an abomination to me. . . .
Wash yourselves; make yourselves clean;
　　remove your evil deeds
　　from before my eyes;
cease to do evil;
　　learn to do good;
seek justice;
　　rescue the oppressed;
defend the orphan;
　　plead for the widow. . . .

Zion shall be redeemed by justice,
　　and those in her who repent, by righteousness.
But rebels and sinners shall be destroyed together,
　　and those who forsake the LORD shall be consumed. . . .
The strong shall become like tinder
　　and their work like a spark;
they and their work shall burn together,
　　with no one to quench them.

The beginning of a book frames the whole, and it is not surprising to find that John drew from many places in the book of Isaiah. Chapter 10 speaks of God wielding an axe against the unrighteous and cutting down trees in the manner that John likewise predicted. Most famously, Isaiah 40:3 was associated with John, connecting his prophetic crying out with the wilderness. John clearly had a strong sense of calling as a prophet, and many of his contemporaries placed him in that category without question, while Jesus of Nazareth went further and said he was even more than a prophet, the greatest human being to ever walk the earth (Matt. 11:9–11 // Luke 7:26–28). Prophets are not complete innovators, however. We see how ideas and phrases were shared and passed down among and between ancient Israel's prophets. It is no surprise that John found inspiration and a framework for his own prophetic activity in the words of prophets who had preceded him.

I referred to words from the first chapter of Isaiah as perhaps having served as John's manifesto. John's own life and activity seem to have been a manifesto for those in his time who shared his dismay at what the people and their worship had become. We might say that John was the living, breathing equivalent of what a particular book has sometimes accomplished in the era of the paperback. There can be lots of desire for change in many quarters, and suddenly a volume appears on the scene that turns these tiny separate flames into one raging fire that transforms a generation.[14] In the era before printing and widespread literacy, rarely if ever did a book play that sort of role. Instead, it was a living voice that accomplished this. It isn't surprising, therefore, that John's impact was remembered in precisely those terms. "A voice crying ... prepare!"

In a later chapter, we will explore his announcement that, as part of the arrival of God's judgment, one stronger than he would appear on the scene, someone who would emerge from among his followers (the phrase "one who comes after me" denoted discipleship, just as we see when Jesus used it). Before we get there, however, we must first consider how he gathered followers and how the diverse groups that he reached and brought together ultimately produced multiple vibrant movements that had very different visions of what it meant to adhere to and promote John's teaching. As we shall see in the next

14. I am indebted to Prof. Jan Dochhorn for suggesting this analogy in a conversation we had about John.

chapter, the bringing together of diverse creative minds around a written man-ifesto, or around the kind of creative personality John clearly was, often gives birth to not just one movement but eventually several, as those innovative thinkers and activists take the initial spark and carry the resulting flame in very different directions.

The Lost Sheep of Israel

W e now have a sense of how John's family background set him on the course to become a revolutionary figure in the realm of religion, and some of the steps he followed as he discerned his vocation and developed a new and innovative ritual. We may presume that John began by immersing himself, by committing to do that which he called others to do, and experienced God in a new and powerful way as a result. The next step was to share what he was doing with others. How did John make disciples? How did he identify and connect with an audience receptive to the message that he felt called to proclaim?

Those whom John influenced directly or indirectly went about proclaiming the good news of the kingdom of God in different ways. Jesus seems to have avoided the biggest cities, focusing instead on smaller towns. The apostle Paul, in contrast, focused his attention on major urban centers, confident that the communities he founded in these regional hubs would then spread the message to surrounding towns and villages. Both preached in synagogues according to the New Testament sources. We are not told in the New Testament that John ever preached in a synagogue or visited a city, but that doesn't mean that he did neither. If you cannot imagine him doing these things, you probably still need to work on shaking the image of John the wild man dressed in animal skins. John was a passionate individual with a great boldness and directness, and at the same time, he was a teacher who gathered students, people who were impressed with what they heard him say and eager to learn more (Luke 3:10–14; John 1:35; 3:25). Eventually, people flocked from far and wide to hear him, and the extent of his influence was remarkable. How did he accomplish this? How did he get there?

Sometimes one must go to the places an individual is associated with to get a feel for the lay of the land. That is no less true in the case of John the Baptist than in the cases of Jesus, Paul, and other figures who are the focus of many organized tours to the Holy Land or Turkey and Greece each year. When I wanted to take a John the Baptist tour, I had to rent a car, book accommodations, and in a few places arrange to speak with an archaeologist who worked on a relevant site. While you can find ready-made tours that promise to let you follow in the footsteps of Jesus or Paul, if you want to focus on the places that are associated with John the Baptist, it will be a do-it-yourself affair. I am not suggesting that any of the aforementioned visits takes you to the places as they were roughly two millennia ago, of course. Places change dramatically over the centuries. Despite the changes that have intervened, however, the places can still speak to us and provide insights, especially if we couple our exploration of those sites with insights from archaeologists who have dug beneath the surface. Without a sense of not only what John did but where he did it, our account of his life will be missing a crucially important piece.

Determined to get as close as I could to the vicinity of where John is supposed to have baptized at Aenon near Salem (John 3:23), I looked online for accommodation in the vicinity of what is today Tel Shalem, the most likely place to correspond to John's Salim (Salem). Tel Shalem is at the location marked as Aenon near Salim on what is quite likely the oldest map of the Holy Land. Made in mosaic, what remains of this map for pilgrims can be seen as part of the floor of Saint George's Church in Madaba, Jordan. Egeria also visited Aenon near Salim in the fourth century and wrote an account of her pilgrimage to the Holy Land that still survives. It is hard to imagine that people once consulted a mosaic map and then set out to find a place like that. I found it challenging enough with the benefit of my phone to guide me as a GPS. The place I stayed is a kibbutz that, I was to discover after arriving, was rarely a destination for foreign tourists. There was a sign taped to a door to indicate where reception was, and occasionally one might find someone there. Despite (and to some extent because of) the challenges of getting there and getting checked in, the place helped to dramatically reshape my understanding of where John had been active, which in turn can reconfigure how we think of his aims as well as of him as a person. The site is extremely remote today. Tel Shalem denotes a large mound of earth beneath which one citadel after another stood over long epochs of time. None of that is visible today. The current landscape and the remoteness of the site today do not reflect the realities that lie hidden beneath the surface, remnants and reminders of what it was like in John's time.

Strolling about the kibbutz, admiring the lush vegetation, the parakeets and the peacock, and the fruit growing in abundance, I eventually found myself at an open-air display of some of the archaeological discoveries made on the site. These included mile markers from the time of Roman emperor Marcus Aurelius. In other words, in the late second century, the Romans built a road right through this area. Roman roads were famous for their straightness and durability and thus sometimes followed more direct routes than had been typical previously. However, they did not pop up in places people did not travel. Even before the Romans built an improved road, we know that people followed the Jordan River valley as one major travel route between Galilee and Jerusalem. Not far to the north of Tel Shalem, less than a three-hour walk, is Beit She'an (Scythopolis), the only city of the Decapolis east of the Jordan River.[1] This enormous urban center is one of the best-preserved ancient cities in the region. One can still visit its massive theater today.

This was John's wilderness. Like the Church of the Temptation on a cliff above the city of Jericho, a major city in John's time as today, the places John was associated with as wilderness were not in the middle of nowhere. On the contrary, they were in the middle of everything, not in but in between and alongside the major urban centers. That is likely why John focused his attention there. A Hellenistic gentile city like those of the Decapolis was not where his primary audience could be found. The place where he could be guaranteed a

---

1. For comparison, this is about the same distance that separated Nazareth from Sep-phoris, the erstwhile capital and leading city of Galilee. Most scholars consider it likely that Jesus and other members of his family made the journey to that city on at least some occasions and perhaps did so regularly. On the location, see Shimon Gibson, "On John the Baptist at the Jordan River: Geohistorical and Archaeological Considerations," in *Fountains of Wisdom: In Conversation with James H. Charlesworth*, ed. Gerbern S. Oegema, Henry W. Morisada Rietz, and Loren T. Stuckenbruck (London: T&T Clark, 2022), 233–36, http:// www.bloomsburycollections.com/book/fountains-of-wisdom-in-conversation-with -james-h-charlesworth/ch15-on-john-the-baptist-at-the-jordan-river-geohistorical-and -archaeological-considerations/; Joan E. Taylor, "John the Baptist on the River Jordan: Localities and Their Significance," *ARAM Periodical* 29 (2017): 371–73.

hearing by the audience he hoped to reach was on the way between the Jewish populations in Galilee and Jerusalem, and at the crossroads that connected Judea and Samaria with the region beyond the Jordan. The Gospel of John says that John baptized at Aenon near Salim (i.e., in Aramaic, the springs near Salem) because "there was much water there" (John 3:23). I had no real sense of what that meant until I stayed at the kibbutz and saw their fish pools stretching for a mile or more, created with water from the springs there. Having so much living water, from springs as well as the river, all in one place, close to a major travel route would have made this a natural place for John to spend time. It was a place where travelers would have stopped, expecting to find water and fruit. People traveling the route from Galilee to Jerusalem would have been primed to appreciate a teacher who said that God was tired of seeing his people imagining that God's presence and his forgiveness were locked up in distant places and dependent on the slaughter of animals. The further they had traveled, the more receptive they might be. It was likely along this route that John made his many disciples from Galilee.

That group, of course, included John's most famous disciple, Jesus from Nazareth. But the Gospel of John also depicts several other individuals from Galilee who would eventually become Jesus's disciples and who were first part of John's movement alongside him (John 1:35–44). The people from Alexandria and Ephesus who had been baptized with John's baptism (Acts 18:24–25; 19:1–3) were people whose difficulty in reaching Jerusalem was far greater than that of Galileans. If not John himself, then other members of his circle would have gone to stand along the routes people followed from those places, proclaiming baptism for the forgiveness of sins as an alternative to sacrifice. John's message was that God was tired of people subscribing to the notion that forgiveness could be obtained only in one location. God was also tired of the notion that people could buy forgiveness (with the possible corollary that the wealthy could afford to sin). The time had come for the promise of the prophets to be fulfilled, that God would sprinkle water on the nation, lead them again through waters, and make them clean. Along the various routes through the wilderness that led to Jerusalem from various other places, John or his representative was waiting, with a message that hit home with pilgrims.

I can't help wondering whether there might not have been an additional reason John was drawn to the springs near Salem. That place called Salem may have been the ancient city of which Melchizedek was king and priest

(Gen. 14:18–20). He met Abraham in a valley that later came to be identified as the Kidron Valley near Jerusalem, but that doesn't necessarily mean that his Salem was the city Jerusalem (although that was later assumed to be the case, or perhaps deliberately promoted by the rulers of Jerusalem).[2] Melchizedek's offering of bread and wine is reminiscent of the rituals of both Mandaeans and Christians. Might John, barred from serving as a Levitical priest, have thought he could be a "priest according to the order of Melchizedek," who could carry out a ritual in river valleys that included those who partook of it sharing bread and wine? The fact that the author of Hebrews connects this with Jesus as he does (Heb. 7, drawing on Ps. 110) may represent one of the many instances of Christians transferring to Jesus things that were first said about John. These texts may have provided yet another scriptural inspiration for John's distinctive way of performing a priestly role outside of the framework and constraints of the Levitical priesthood, one that connects with a specific wilderness place where John is known to have been active.

While John certainly drew disciples by speaking to passersby, that may not be how he started. While only the Gospel of Luke (and later sources dependent on it) records that John and Jesus were related, we should not be too quick to dismiss this information. In this ancient Mediterranean cultural context, family networks were the very fabric of social life. Note how the followers of John and later of Jesus included siblings, and that Jesus's followers and supporters included parents of some of his disciples. Nothing much was ever accomplished impersonally, unlike the ways many of us are used to doing things today. No one would put up a "help wanted" or "disciples wanted" sign on a local bulletin board and then conduct interviews. Whether one was seeking a craftsman for a project or starting a religious movement, relatives were the place one started. If John left home still at odds with his father, that doesn't mean his mother, Elizabeth, would not have sought to connect him with relatives who could help him. It may be for that reason that it is Elizabeth's relatives but not Zechariah's that are associated with John's movement. Family connections must have been part of the picture, particularly in the very early stages of John's preparations for his public activity. When John first

---

2. On this, see Robert R. Cargill, *Melchizedek, King of Sodom: How Scribes Invented the Biblical Priest-King* (New York: Oxford University Press, 2019), 56–59, https://doi.org/10.1093/oso/9780190946968.001.0001.

stationed himself by the river seeking to connect with pilgrims traveling from Galilee along the Jordan River's Rift Valley to Jerusalem, he almost certainly had at least a few compatriots with him. Once that was in place, he and his initial core group could position themselves along the major thoroughfare that followed the river and proclaim their message. There John found a ready stream (pun intended) of people whose very journey meant they cared about worship and yet who were primed to recognize the unfairness that worship was less accessible and costlier for some than for others because of that journey they were making.

FISHING FOR SOULS/PEOPLE

Although we regularly turn in this book to the evidence from Jesus to help us get a clearer view of John, the depiction of Jesus calling disciples in the Synoptic Gospels is unlikely to help us here. Those stories have often been read as accounts of Jesus encountering complete strangers and, through sheer force of his personality or raw spiritual magnetism, having them leave everything and follow Jesus after just a few words. As we have already discussed, the Gospel of John clues us in that in fact Jesus already knew those Galilean fishermen, and likely also tax collectors like Levi, from John's entourage (John 1:40–45). When Jesus approached them in Galilee, it was not a first meeting. Presumably the followers of John had scattered back to their homes after John's arrest. Not long after, Jesus approached some of them to regroup them. The words he used when he did so likely echoed some of John's sayings and teaching. When Jesus said he would make these individuals who worked in the fishing industry "fishers for people," that image finds a close parallel in the Mandaean Book of John 36–39. There an extended parable is told about a figure who is mistaken initially for an ordinary fisherman but who is revealed to be one who fishes for souls. At one climactic point, we read,

> I am a fisher of the souls who bear witness to Life. I am a fisher who summons the poor, gathers them together, and gives them hope, who calls them and tells them, "come gather by my side," who tells them, "If you come, wanderers, you will be saved from the crafty birds. I shall save my friends, raise them up, set them in my vessel, dress them in splendid gar-

ments, and cover them in precious light. . . . They will sit on thrones and
shine forth with precious light. I shall take them and rise up, and you, the
Seven (planets), will stay here. The fate of scum and filth will be your fate.
The day of light shall rise, and the darkness shall return to its place. I and
my disciples shall rise, and we shall see light's place." (36:87–99)[3]

You will likely have noticed some striking similarities to language Jesus
used in reference to discipleship. There are also resonances with other things
Jesus said, about his inner circle of followers sitting enthroned, for instance, as
well as with the imagery of light and darkness most distinctive of the Gospel
of John. Why is that language also to be found in a Mandaean text? Most likely
because John the Baptist used it. It is hard to imagine someone who looked
more like a "fisher for people" than John did, as he stood in the water and called
people to repent and undergo baptism. When Jesus used that phrase, he was
deliberately echoing John's language. Jesus was regrouping John's followers
around himself. By echoing John's language in his call to them to follow him,
Jesus was saying, "Join me—John's work is going to continue, and we are going to continue it." If Jesus was regrouping John's followers in these accounts,
then we should not imagine John's initial gathering of disciples as occurring
in precisely the same way.

We have little concrete information about how, if at all, John's movement
was organized. The same is also true, for the most part, of the Jesus movement
that followed after it. What little we know about the latter, however, can help
us to understand the former. Both appear to have involved a central figure,
a core of learners, and a larger host of people who embraced the message and
sought forgiveness through immersion and were thus part of the movement
in the wider sense. We cannot use the forms that Christianity and Mandaeism
later took as a guide to the movement in its early days, because as far as we can
tell, there was no effort yet to create a community with a distinct identity from
the wider Jewish community. Those baptized by John were already part of a
community. They belonged to a people, the people of Israel, and that people
was the focus of John's message. It was only later that these groups would

3. Based on the translation in Charles G. Häberl and James F. McGrath, *The Mandaean
Book of John: Critical Edition, Translation, and Commentary* (Berlin: de Gruyter, 2019),
https://doi.org/10.1515/9783110487862.

organize meetings of their own independent of existing synagogue and other local community structures.

The message of John was an apocalyptic one, in the sense that he expected radical change after which nothing would be the same. That change could take one of two forms, depending on how people responded to his message. It could be a disaster for the entire people of Israel, with God's agent carrying out judgment against them. If enough people responded to John's message by turning their lives around, however, it could be a time when the unrighteous would be purged from the nation and the people would be led into a glorious future that surpassed anything in the nation's past. Many historians have contrasted John and Jesus by casting the former as more strongly apocalyptic than the latter. In fact, this was a point of continuity between them. Yet in referring to John as someone who expected a dramatic upheaval in the near future, we need not imagine that John expected that change to occur solely by miraculous divine action, while human beings simply watched passively. As we explore in the next chapter, John predicted that he would have a successor from among his disciples who would act more forcefully than he himself had, who would bring about the winnowing that he predicted. Like so many prophets before him, John was not merely predicting the future. Through his words, he was contributing to bringing that future into existence.

We need to add some additional comments about what discipleship meant. The terminology has largely fallen out of use except in the context of Christianity, where discipleship has more to do with worship than education. Jesus and other disciples of John were his apprentices, there to learn his way of life and his teaching through instruction and emulation. The community that formed around John, and in particular those whom he admitted to his inner circle to train and authorize to represent him in other places, might perhaps be compared to a graduate seminar. If that isn't a familiar image from your experience, then imagine a cross between a regular book club and the occasional neighborhood meeting to address a specific problem. If none of these analogies is helpful, don't worry, since ancient education and discipleship aren't quite like any of these modern things, and so analogies can go only so far and risk misleading us if we read too much of our own experience into the lives of ancient people. The point is that learning happened with a teacher whose insights were held in high esteem, and it happened through vigorous discussions rather than passive lecturing. When people trained with a rabbi, they did so to become rabbis themselves. Even that terminology can be misleading, since in that era, there was nothing like ordination. Those who studied the Jewish sacred texts and received tips on how to expound them might preach sermons in synagogues, but that was not a full-time job. That same training enabled them to serve as what the Bible sometimes translates as "lawyers," but which meant something different in the absence of a modern judicial system. What is similar is that they studied the relevant laws and the history of how they were interpreted and applied.

For John, however, the details of how to apply the laws in the torah do not appear to have been his focus. When John talks about righteousness, he comments on matters that are not addressed in so many words in the Scriptures. There is no law requiring someone with two shirts to give one to someone who has none. Neither was there any law addressing tax collectors and soldiers not using their positions to enrich themselves (Luke 3:10–14). John explicitly differentiated himself from others. He was a teacher of righteousness but not like the figure who bore that title in the Dead Sea Scrolls. He was not focused on getting people to be more rigorously pure or even on how to navigate tensions between different laws in torah. Such debates could easily distract from rather than enhance basic fairness.

When Jesus emphasized these points in his ethical teaching, he most likely was not simply repeating exactly what John said, at least for the most part. But the gist, the essence of it, was what John taught. Some of John's students may have gone back to their local communities and become teachers in them, disseminating his teaching that way. Most probably did not. Some accompanied him and represented him, as we also see later when Jesus sent out apostles to proclaim his message and further his work. Some, as again we see in the case of those who encountered Jesus, had a brief encounter with John, underwent baptism, then returned to their homes with a story to tell and an experience to share. Through all these means, John's message and teaching spread, and we can tell from the historical evidence that it did so effectively.

A New People or a People Made New?

One key element in John's message was his emphasis on the impossibility of relying on ancestry, on belonging to a people group descended from Abraham, as though that meant that one would not be held accountable for wrongdoing

(Matt. 3:9 // Luke 3:8). This was not a new idea that John had come up with. Far from it. It was, in fact, the central emphasis of most of ancient Israel's prophets (see, e.g., Amos 3:2; 9:7; Jer. 9:11–26). Yet it was and is something surprisingly easy to forget. If we look at how the apostle Paul's development of John's idea has been reinterpreted within Christianity, it becomes clearer how this can happen. In chapter 3 of his letter to the Romans, Paul emphasizes that it would make God unjust if God simply let a particular people off the hook. It would also be unjust if God let the fact that people have been circumcised, and thus that they have joined the covenant with Abraham, mean that they can get away with murder, literally or metaphorically. Paul thus emphasized that God would judge all people, Jews and gentiles, by what they had done, and would consider righteous those who were characterized by faithfulness, as Abraham had been. In all of this, Paul was building on a foundation that John laid. That many Christians have understood Paul to be saying that Christians are saved no matter what they do, while everyone else goes to hell, illustrates how one can have direct challenges to this sort of reliance on group belonging in one's Scriptures and yet nonetheless adopt precisely the stance that those Scriptures argue against. That had happened in the era John was living in as well, and he took it upon himself to address it.

There is a direct line running from John through Jesus to Paul when it comes to this particular theme. Paul may be a further step removed from John than Jesus was, a disciple of John's disciple, but that doesn't mean he cannot be helpful in fleshing out what John had to say. There is another reason why it is important to mention Paul in this context. Paul is famous for having welcomed gentiles into the people of God, contributing to the rupture that resulted in Christianity becoming a separate world religion, and one that is predominantly non-Jewish. John did not take his views on the unimportance of ancestry that far.[4] His message was not that the axe was at the root of the tree, singular, ready to cut down the nation and make a fresh start with another people, but that the axe was at the root of the trees, that each individual would be held accountable and no individual would escape based on what earlier generations had done (Matt. 3:10 // Luke 3:9).

---

4. Luke presents Jesus as referring to Elijah's and Elisha's assistance to non-Israelites. Elijah serves as a pattern for the inclusion of foreigners, and this could not fail to have John in mind given his deliberate emulation of Elijah.

While Paul would view gentiles as becoming children of Abraham through God's miraculous agency, branches grafted into the tree of Israel, John's aim was to convey something to his fellow Israelites. Among other things, they should be reminded that they were just a subset of the descendants of Abraham. When John said that God could raise up children for Abraham from the stones, it was not just a reference to the miraculous power of God to do the impossible, or simply a pun (the words for sons and stones in Aramaic are similar). The point was that there were children of Abraham in every direction, whether he was on the end of the Jordan closer to Lake Tiberias or the end closer to the Dead Sea, who were not part of the covenant. There were children of Abraham living in the stony regions of Transjordan, including Nabataeans, Edomites, and also Israelites who preserved traditions at odds with torah. Whether he happened to be standing at a place where to the west of the Jordan lay Samaria or Judea, each of those groups felt the other had gone astray and perhaps weren't even really Israelites at all. Were all of them fine as they were as Abraham's descendants, or were they proof that being descendants of Abraham was not enough? If claiming Abraham as ancestor was enough, why did so many Jews not embrace Samaritans as their kin, to say nothing of Idumeans and Arabs? John challenged his contemporaries to ask what should constitute the identity of the people of God, what, if anything, made the children of Abraham special (and a subset of them perhaps even more so). John was convinced that if Abraham's children actually came together in righteousness, God would be pleased with any of them that did so. Instead, they were locked in debates about which of them was most correct and most beloved in God's sight.

For John, what made a difference was not ancestry but the covenant, and the covenant came with responsibilities and not only privileges. "Covenant" is just a fancy term for relationship with obligations. John emphasized that God had made a nation with a covenant, not a covenant with a nation. In other words, God had singled out Abraham and his descendants for receipt of a covenant, but from the very beginning, Abraham's household did not necessarily include only his biological kin (Gen. 17:9–14). Fast-forward to the exodus from Egypt, and we read of a ragtag mixed group of mostly but not exclusively Hebrews exiting Egypt (Exod. 12:38). Foreigners, it was assumed, would always be found among the people of God and participate in their worship and their righteousness. This was a perennial theme from the patriarchal narratives about marriages all the way to the story of exodus and beyond. The laws in torah likewise envisaged people living in Israel and participating as resident aliens within the framework of the covenant. God had entrusted Israel with something special, not so that they could claim it was theirs and theirs alone, much less rely on it as though it excused their misdeeds rather than demanded their faithfulness and uprightness. The covenant and its commandments were meant so that they could show the world a different way of being. If they failed, the fact that they had received the covenant would make things worse for them, not better. That is the point many of ancient Israel's prophets had made, and it was echoed by John, and then Jesus, and then Paul, to name just a couple of the many whom John influenced directly and indirectly.

While John may not have gone as far as Paul did in negating the importance of differences between Israel and the nations, that is not the only distinction between human beings that Paul mentions. He also lists male and female alongside Jew and Greek, slave and free (Gal. 3:28). On the subject of gender equality, John does seem to have led the way and not merely articulated a principle that others after him would take further than he himself did. He may have owed something of this insight to his mother, who supported John and utilized her family connections to help him when he stood against his father's wishes for him. Joanna may also have been one of his supporters and, after his imprisonment, continued her support by directing it to Jesus as the new leader of the movement.

The sons of Zebedee are also supposed to have been disciples of John initially, and their mother's involvement in Jesus's movement suggests that she, too, was probably involved from the time they were all connected with John. An early Jewish-Christian gospel records that Mary was the one who heard about John's baptism and took her sons to be baptized.[5] It is perhaps noteworthy that even for Paul, it was through baptism (which for him meant incorporation "in Christ") that distinctions between male and female were rendered of no importance. Note as well the way Matthew 21:31–32 mentions not only tax collectors but also prostitutes as those who responded to John's

---

5. This text is sometimes called the Gospel of the Nazarenes, at other times the Gospel according to the Hebrews. At times, it is not clear whether we are dealing with one work or two, since we know of it, or them, only through quotations by early Christian authors. This particular detail is mentioned by Jerome in his work *Against Pelagius* 3.2.

message.[6] In view of what was considered appropriate in this ancient context in terms of physical contact between men and women who were not related or married, if John's baptism involved him or his representative actively dunking or laying hands on the baptized person, then he may well have had a wife or female followers, or both, who did this for women who were baptized. John's movement attracted men and women, and we have reason to think that both women and men played leading roles in it.

PROSTITUTES AND TAX COLLECTORS

None of the places where we are told John was active seems a likely place for him to interact with either tax collectors or prostitutes. Yet the Gospel of Matthew says he found a receptive audience in both groups (21:28–32). This may hint at John being more widely traveled than we have record of. Wherever we locate his opportunities to be heard by prostitutes and tax collectors, the harsh tone he adopted toward self-assured religious leaders was undoubtedly not the one he used when addressing these others. The impression people

6. On the need for women to perform baptism and anointing of women, see Joan E. Taylor, "Two by Two: The Ark-Etypal Language of Mark's Apostolic Pairings," in *The Body in Biblical, Christian and Jewish Texts*, ed. Joan E. Taylor, Library of Second Temple Studies (London: Bloomsbury T&T Clark, 2014), 69–70. Mandaean tradition records that John was married. It is difficult to know whether this is historical. As has been pointed out in relation to the question of whether Jesus was married, absence of mention of a wife in this patriarchal context cannot serve as evidence that someone was unmarried. On the other hand, his rather unusual childhood and relationship with his father makes it seem rather unlikely that a marriage would have been arranged for him. The fact that her name, according to chapter 31 of the Book of John, was Anhar, which means "rivers," perhaps suggests that this is legend rather than history, or even something that started off with a figurative meaning ("he is married to rivers") and came to be understood literally at some later point. The fact that Jesus touched women when he healed them may also suggest a willingness to have physical contact with the opposite sex, or perhaps that our assumptions about physical contact taboos in the era are incorrect. On the history of women baptizing in Christianity, see Ally Kateusz, *Mary and Early Christian Women: Hidden Leadership* (Cham, Switzerland: Springer International, 2019), https://doi.org/10.1007/978-3-030-11111-3. The connection of John with both Christianity and Gnosticism (on which see below), coupled with the existence of women who baptized and had positions of authority in both traditions at least initially, suggests this goes back to John.

have of John as someone who was harsh and stern is based on what he said to members of the religious elite, whom he teased and castigated as hypocrites. Even in criticizing them, we see his penchant for sarcasm, for wordplay. For John to have made the impact he did on so many different people, and for John to have brought together the truly diverse people we hear were part of his movement, he would have had to be a charming individual, one with a disarming persona and wit, as well as a passionate one capable of seriousness and severity. Although Jesus would be the one to earn the label as a result of his practice of accepting invitations to their homes, we should not fail to recognize the extent to which "friend of tax collectors and sinners" would have been equally applicable to his mentor John (Luke 5:27–32; Matt. 11:19).

The very fact that John approached prostitutes and tax collectors at all, never mind that he did so in a friendly and compassionate manner, would have made an impression on them. To figure out what his gospel was for these specific categories of people and why he made such an impact on them in particular, we need to ask what they had in common. Neither set of people would have classified themselves as similar to the other. I imagine John may well have grabbed the attention of prostitutes and tax collectors by highlighting to each the ways in which they were like the other. Both would have been offended. It is jarring to see one's resemblance to a category of people one despises. But it can be effective, if the aim is to provoke reflection and ultimately change. Prostitutes and tax collectors were people who, in different ways, managed to cope financially in the exploitative system within which they lived, by doing things that (when things went in their favor) could bring them a measure of financial security others lacked but in the process also marginalized them forever.

Chief tax collectors paid for the right to collect the taxes due by fronting that money and then collecting what people owed, plus more on top as profit for themselves. When we are told that tax collectors responded to John, it has those who worked for the chief tax collectors in mind, rather than their bosses. Most individuals in this line of work would be people who had failed to find other employment and were willing to accept the stigma of playing a role in this system, one that everyone hated because it took already burdensome taxation and made it worse.

Prostitutes could be upper-class women who fell into financial difficulty but were more often slaves or former slaves. None of them would have had any real choice about their work. Yet they would have been viewed not as victims of an un-

just economic system but as sexually promiscuous women with insatiable appe-
tites.[7] They knew better. Even household slaves were liable to be used and abused
by their owners for sexual purposes, and so being forced into prostitution was only
one of many ways that women were exploited in that era. Prostitutes were, on the
other hand, sometimes able to keep a part of their earnings, which was more than
could be said of most slaves. That meant the prospect of eventually buying their
freedom, or at least living somewhat better than others did from day to day.

People in both these professions were better poised than anyone in that
time to see how the system exploited them and, at the same time, pushed them
to exploit others in the interest of protecting themselves and trying to ensure
their own well-being. John asked them to envisage a different world and what
it would take to make it a reality. That it was not something that any individual
could accomplish on their own hints at the way John's message by its very na-
ture brought a community into existence, one that sought to provide support
as they sought to live in this new way.

Soldiers and tax collectors were people who worked for others who en-
riched themselves through extortion. They often used the authority they had
in that role to do likewise. What did it mean when John instructed tax collectors to take only what they were ordered to (Luke 3:13)? Presumably much
the same as is said to the soldiers (3:14): be content with what you are paid.
Those in both these jobs are told to accept their wage and not seek to acquire
further income by using their position of relative authority over others to lay
claim to what is not theirs, not owed to them.[8] To settle for their wage meant
forgoing a buffer against starvation in a world where that was a constant risk.
It meant accepting that risk not only for themselves but also for their families.
The alternative was to try to make your situation better by making the situation
of others even more perilous. At the core of John's teaching on this subject
was this: not allowing the experience of being exploited to turn you into an
exploiter of others, not making victims of others in the interest of avoiding
having a similar fate befall yourself.

---

7. On this subject, see Anise K. Strong, *Prostitutes and Matrons in the Roman World*
(Cambridge: Cambridge University Press, 2016).

8. The language of Lev. 19 pops up here again, as similar terminology is found in 19:11, as
noted by François Bovon, *Luke 1: A Commentary on the Gospel of Luke 1:1–9:50*, trans. Christine M. Thomas (Minneapolis: Fortress, 2002), 124, https://doi.org/10.2307/j.ctvb6v878.

When we look closely at the things we are told about John's teaching to people in these specific lines of work, we realize once again how much of Jesus's teaching stems from John. John's core message was about treating others the way you wanted to be treated. In practice, it involved giving up what you had for the sake of others, in the interest of a kingdom that was hoped for, one where the exploitation they had experienced and the exploitation they had perpetrated would be no more. None of them on their own could bring that way of doing things to an end. The most that could be done was to refuse to play an unjust part in it any longer, and to hunger and thirst for the justice of God's kingdom. This is surely the hardest for those who have suffered at the hands of an unjust system. Yet John started there, and got a hearing. People who had faced fewer hardships than they had and had never had to sacrifice their reputation in the interest of survival were less receptive of John's message and continued to look down on those categories of people for whom John's message resonated most strongly. That John was empathetic to those he called to repentance is made clearest by the fact that he did not call them to leave their only source of livelihood, only to deal fairly on the level of their own individual acts and choices. John was passionate about justice, but he recognized that injustice was something systemic and not something that could be blamed on prostitutes and tax collectors while the wealthy elite escaped accusation. It took wealth to be able to afford to give the appearance of keeping one's hands clean. In reality, everyone lives entangled in an unjust system. The elite of John's time might perhaps be compared to those who take pride in buying fair-trade and environmentally friendly products, while the systems that exploit the poor and the earth continue unchallenged. Then as now, people profit from an unjust system and salve their conscience by giving a bit from their extensive surplus to help others.

I suspect that one of John's aims in his time in the wilderness, as he lived on food that came to him with no need to pay or cultivate, was an experiment in practicing justice. I have sometimes thought it would be worth writing a book with a title like *A Year of Living Justly*. I haven't pursued it, because even the thought of what would be involved is too daunting. There is no way I could tell how every item of food and clothing, every piece of technology, did or did not involve someone being paid unfairly, some natural resource being exploited. John, living in the wilderness, went to the furthest extreme possible in extricating himself from the tangled web of injustice in his society. While in the wilderness fending for himself and relying on what God provided, he owed nothing to anyone, and no one owed him anything. Yet the wider society carried on, in no way challenged or changed as a result of his individual justice. I am convinced that motivated John to come back and proclaim the need to change individually and as a society, while at the same time giving him empathy and a tolerance for the fact that no person who did not leave everything and go to the wilderness could be without sin.[9] There should thus be no casting of stones, no denunciation except of those who refused to recognize their own individual and collective guilt. Even as guidance to people in society, however, he could emphasize the way God provided for plants and animals, and that there was a need to let go of worry—not as an end in itself but because it was worry that most frequently motivated people to seek more, to build walls and financial buffers that took from others to make themselves feel safer and more secure. John felt called not to achieve an illusion of personal purity but to risk returning to society and getting his hands dirty in order to challenge the very order of things, this taken-for-granted fabric of society itself. He did so always clad in his stereotypical camel cloth, an outward symbol of constant repentance.

A FAITHFUL REMNANT

As John focused his activity along thoroughfares in the countryside, and perhaps even earlier when he was in the wilderness figuring out what life would

9. James R. Edwards, *The Gospel according to Luke*, Pillar New Testament Commentary (Grand Rapids: Eerdmans, 2015), 113, writes, "One can fairly ask how tax collectors and soldiers could comply with John's commands. John does not ground his commands in Torah or rabbinic tradition. Unlike Judaism before and the early church after, he does not require tax collectors and soldiers to desist or be rejected. He does not require them to leave occupations and workplaces where there are moral compromises, to practice pacifism, or to retreat into religious insularity. John grounds his commands in self-evident moral standards. His instructions assume that, even in difficult and compromising circumstances, there are ways to behave decently and morally. He does not expect the crowds, tax collectors, and soldiers to change social structures, but, like yeast and leaven, to humanize them by just and honorable behavior. John's counsel anticipates Jesus's quintessential moral maxim, 'Do to others as you would have them do to you' (6:31)." See also I. Howard Marshall, *The Gospel of Luke*, New International Commentary on the New Testament (Grand Rapids: Eerdmans, 1978), 142–44.

have in store for him, he had opportunities to intersect not only with travelers between major cities and towns but also people from more remote villages. While dramatic changes and cultural exchange tend to happen in urban centers if and when such things occur, remote areas often preserve traditional ways of life even when the rest of society is shifting in a new direction. This is true not only when it comes to handicrafts or music but also religion.

While most people today have heard the word "pagan," what far fewer are aware of is that it comes from a Latin word that originally denoted someone from the countryside. It came to mean someone who doesn't embrace Christianity at least in part because, as Christianity became more and more influential in the Roman Empire in the major urban areas, the centers of power and authority, those in more distant places were not always quick to follow suit. Indeed, some who lived in remote villages would have missed the memo entirely. Even if your remote hamlet got wind that major changes were happening in other parts of the empire, that wasn't necessarily a reason for you and your neighbors to change your traditional ways of doing things.[10] No one was going to go village by village looking for people who did not take their traditional gods and rituals and immediately toss them in the trash.

A similar process happened among the ancient Israelites. After the Babylonians destroyed Jerusalem and carried off significant numbers of people from the kingdom of Judah, the Persian king Cyrus allowed people to return. Scriptures were compiled and codified, and an effort was made to promote the elimination of rural places of worship in favor of centralization in Jerusalem. In some places, it was only during the era of Hasmonean rule, in the second century BC, that we see the observance of torah really taking hold.[11] Even then, the people who had maintained ancient Israelite religious traditions, including adherence to multiple deities, did not simply vanish. In some out-of-the-way places, they may have been able to continue business as usual. In others, however, they saw that there was a real threat against them if they continued. So they went underground (metaphorically, obviously), maintaining their views

10. James Joseph O'Donnell, *Pagans: The End of Traditional Religion and the Rise of Christianity* (New York: HarperCollins, 2015), 159–64. For uncertainties about the connotations of the term when adopted by Christians, see Alan Cameron, *The Last Pagans of Rome* (New York: Oxford University Press, 2010), 14–25.

11. On this, see in particular Yonatan Adler, *The Origins of Judaism: An Archaeological-Historical Reappraisal* (New Haven: Yale University Press, 2022).

and practices in secret as they perceived that those in authority increasingly viewed them negatively. In particular, they developed their own satirical way of interpreting the Scriptures that had been introduced in their community and imposed on them. When the creator God claimed to be the only God (Deut. 32:39; Isa. 46:9), they imagined a voice from further up the chain of divinity mocking the ignorance and hubris of such an assertion. These views would emerge into public view as they became part of the religious tradition that is most commonly known under the label "Gnosticism."

Most people have at least heard of Gnosticism and gnostics, but the most distinctive and characteristic viewpoint associated with that label nevertheless remains unfamiliar. The ancient gnostics were quite diverse but mostly agreed on this point, viewing the creator deity as an inferior being far removed from the supreme source of all. The idea that the material world might owe its existence to a cosmic mistake by some lower being can seem quite surprising to those used to affirming one God as supreme and creator of all. Yet that is what the ancient gnostics believed.

Even less well known than these points of doctrine is the association of Gnosticism with John the Baptist via certain individuals who are supposed to have been part of his movement: Simon and Dositheus. They were from Samaria, one of the areas most resistant to the imposition of rule by Jerusalem and that had existed for centuries as an independent kingdom known as Israel, which overshadowed her smaller southern neighbor economically and politically. As John spent time in Samaria and its vicinity, he was heard not only by people who shared most of his core beliefs and assumptions but also by people who did not. Some of them differed only on questions such as whether worship should be offered on Mount Gerizim or in Jerusalem. John said either, both, or neither. As his follower Jesus is reported to have said, the time was coming and even now has arrived when people will worship in spirit and truth, in connection with living water, so that neither Mount Gerizim nor Jerusalem will be the focus (John 4:21–24). As much as such answers may have irked the priestly elite in Judea and Samaria alike, they were welcome and probably exciting for those who fostered resentment toward the centralization of worship and the associated effort to eliminate traditional religious beliefs and practices.

It is not clear how much John may or may not have become aware of such views held by some of his hearers. He himself, to be clear, did not espouse the views that are distinctive of Gnosticism. Yet his message that torah was not perfect, that worship could occur anywhere, and that an inner spiritual and moral transformation was what really mattered made him seem like a potential ally. They embraced his baptism and other aspects of his teaching, while integrating these things into their subversive take on the Jewish Scriptures. Eventually the result would emerge into public view as what we know as Gnosticism. It seems to have spread most vigorously in precisely those places where people of Israelite ancestry were to be found that lay furthest from the influence from Jerusalem. Thus it was that Samaria, Egypt, and Mesopotamia became the focal points of vibrant gnostic religious groups, one of which—the Mandaeans—persists to the present day.

While it is not entirely clear to what extent John was aware of the full extent of diverse theological perspectives that his followers brought with them, some things he clearly was aware of. In some cases, he engaged with the differences, while in others, he may have considered them matters on which it was possible to disagree. One example is the importance of where one worships. Ultimately some of his followers retained their allegiance to either Jerusalem or Gerizim, if the later movements that emerged from among his followers are anything to go by. Even so, all of them at least relativized the importance of a temple or city by promoting John's baptism. As for the idea that there were multiple divine entities, and it was an inferior one that was responsible for the creation and oversight of the material world, that might not have been as difficult to tolerate as you might imagine. The idea that there was one supreme God, and an array of subordinate entities that emerged from that ultimate creative source, was a point that was shared in common among ancient people. So too was the idea that the world humans inhabit is under the sway of malevolent forces.

Through the group that John gathered around himself, and the diverse movements that emerged after his death, John shows himself to have been an incredibly tolerant individual when it came to what we would classify as theological ideas. John saw that, for all their focus on identifying the right place of worship, on affirming certain axioms as true, Jews, Samaritans, and any others who shared Israelite heritage were united in one thing, namely, a failure to emphasize and live out justice. Yet such things are key concerns in the Torah and the Prophets. John gathered around himself people who shared a range of different viewpoints on many matters and came from an array of backgrounds. When they came to him, he did not ask them to adopt a creed but to repent and commit to cultivating righteousness in the personal sphere and working toward justice in the way they interact with others. He also called at least his core associates to join him in proclaiming this message to their contemporaries.

A CREATIVE CIRCLE

Even though it may not have been highly organized, John was definitely the leader of a movement. In no sense was he a lone hermit figure, one that we would then have to imagine a surprisingly large number of individuals independently admired and sought to emulate. John gathered around himself some of the most creative minds of his era. Jesus of Nazareth obviously falls into this category. We have been mentioning Jesus in passing throughout this biography of John, always aware that Jesus would go on to become so famous and make such an impact on history that he tends to block John from view if he remains in the picture for too long. Hopefully by this point in our life of the Baptist, it will be clear that the impact of Jesus on history deserves to be viewed as at the same time the impact of John through one of his most ardent supporters. And while many have sought a glimpse of the historical John the Baptist out of a desire to bring Jesus into clearer focus, one key distinctive aspect of this life of John, which enabled us to write a biography where others before have felt it could not be done, is the recognition of just how much Jesus of Nazareth informs us about John, if only we take the time to ask and to look.

Some of Jesus's circle of supporters encountered him in the context of John's movement, as we have seen. They, too, appear to have been individuals of some vision and imagination in their own right. To this list, we must add the individual or group that had the idea to interpret John's baptism in light of their ancient Israelite heritage that rejected torah and the supremacy of the creator deity, to couple it with an emphasis on mystical experience, and to integrate elements of Greek philosophy. The early church would identify the key individual in question as a man named Simon from Samaria. Christian tradition starting with the book of Acts would label him Simon Magus, Simon the Magician, or Simon the Magian. It is unfortunate that we do not have sympathetic sources about him. The polemical depictions of him as a fraudulent trickster hungry for self-aggrandizement are not that different from the polemical portraits of Jesus we find in ancient literature hostile to Christianity, and we should treat them with the same skepticism and suspicion. Even if those sources are right about his motives or wrong about his name, or both, there can be no doubt that whoever saw in John's message and rite an opportunity to proclaim this secretive ancestral faith of theirs to a wider audience must have been someone with an impressive combination of imagination and courage. This is true regardless of whether you agree with or profoundly detest their viewpoint.

In recent centuries, we find new and creative movements gathering around natural leaders and sources of inspiration in places like coffeehouses. Such places did not exist in John's time, and it is pointless to speculate whether John's followers might have met there if the possibility had existed (and what impact they might have had on the world with the addition of caffeine into the mix). The analogy is worth making even so, if only to once again force us away from the notion of John as a lone hermit to whom individuals like Jesus related each separately from one another. Instead, we should imagine meetings by a campfire, vigorous debates and exchanges of ideas, as a gathering of people we would recognize as storytellers, poets, and visionaries all found inspiration in John's teaching, the experience of God he promoted and fostered, and the community he was bringing into existence.

While the imagery of John as a lone voice crying in the wilderness speaks in a powerful way to modern individualists, that clearly is not what John was like. Nor, for that matter, is anyone really like that even in our time. While John did not build an organization even in an extended ancient sense of that word, he attracted an entourage of thinkers and activists, and it is implausible to imagine him simply telling them what to do and what he would do. When John criticized Antipas, when he turned his attention to a new geographic region and sent representatives there, lively discussions about the best course of action would have taken place first among John and his closest confidants. This point is not unique to John. Some in our time tend to mistakenly think of key figures from Martin Luther to Martin Luther King Jr. and from Muhammad to Mohandas Gandhi as unilaterally influencing other people and changing the course of history. We know from the sources that we have about each of them that they had trusted advisors, people who influenced them as well as people whom they influenced.

If John left home and managed to survive for some time on food that could be found, learning that God would provide for him as for the animals, he was not a shipwreck survivor on a deserted island. Even the monastics that exemplify what it means to be a recluse are part of a network and create a community. Indeed, even someone like Simeon the Stylite, the monk who became famous for sitting atop a pillar as an extreme expression of his ascetic withdrawal from ordinary life, had regular visitors.

On my John the Baptist Holy Land trip, I made a point of going to Saint George's Monastery in Wadi Qelt not far from Jericho. I did so not because there is a connection with John the Baptist but because it exemplifies the monastic tradition and so many view John through the lens of that way of life. This monastery is well off the highway, reachable via some well-paved but nonetheless extremely twisty roads. The monastery is built up the side of a wadi, that is, a ravine that is dry except occasionally in the rainy season. It seems the epitome of seclusion. Yet as soon as you reach the spot that provides the best view, you are met not by breathtaking isolation but by Bedouin selling trinkets. Even there, one is not truly alone. The monastery welcomes visitors and always has throughout its history. There would have been many more of those in the past. While it is some way from the main driving route today, the Roman road between Jerusalem and Jericho (yes, the famous one from Jesus's story about the Samaritan helping a victim of robbers) ran right along there. Those who sought isolation did not, for the most part, venture that far from populated areas. They went just far enough to get some distance, while remaining close enough to not sever the connection entirely.

More importantly, we have seen throughout this book that John was not that sort of figure. He was no monastic hermit. While he may have sought solitude from time to time, his life was characterized not by withdrawal from people but by engagement with them. In his time between leaving home and appearing on the public scene, he will have had mentors, conversation partners, and others with whom to interact, individuals about whom, alas, we have no information but whose presence in John's life we must posit nonetheless. We can detect their impact, even if only vaguely. Those years of early adulthood turned him into someone who could cope on his own, to be sure, but also turned him into an extremely powerful and effective communicator and leader. That simply doesn't happen living in complete isolation from others. We can deduce important things about John's younger years from his adult life. His experience did not turn him into someone who relied on no one, but someone who saw the value in others and found ways to bring out and nurture that potential.

This life of John is titled *Christmaker*, and John's prediction of a stronger one still to come will be the focus of the next chapter. In the present context, what we need to pay attention to is the fact that John, in a culture in which honor was prized, protected, and fought for, predicted that one who comes after him—that is, one of his own disciples—would be stronger than he, one whose sandals he was not fit to carry or untie (the Gospels differ on the precise expression). Jesus's teaching about humility, it would seem, is also something that he got from or at least shared in common with John. While there were plenty of instances of teachers being overshadowed by their students in the ancient Mediterranean world, few teachers actively expected and encouraged it. If humility, genuinely fostering the success and growth of others, is rare in our time, it would have stood out even more in John's time. Perhaps this offers a new slant on the statement attributed to the Baptist in the Gospel of John, "he must increase, but I must decrease" (3:30). While historians are right to perceive this as the perspective of a Christian author crafting dialogue to make John point away from himself and to Jesus, that doesn't mean it represented a radical revision of history. Spin can take many forms, dramatic and subtle. If John could expect one of his disciples to be stronger than he, a saying like that from the Gospel of John might not be at odds with the personality of the historical John the Baptist, even if the words are not ones he actually uttered.

John had wondered in his younger days what life could possibly have in store for a Nazirite priest. The answer he found to that question was that he was a prophet called to point out the shortcomings of the institutions in which his people placed their hope, and to lead them onto the path of righteousness. Just do what is right, treat others as you would be treated—ideas so simple and yet at the same time so difficult to put into practice consistently. If Herod Antipas and others marveled at the sway John held over crowds, how much more must John have been surprised by how successful he was in getting a hearing for his message and getting people to respond? We are told that tax collectors and prostitutes responded. We are told of soldiers showing that they were aware of the moral issues with which their careers were entangled and sought John's guidance. Those who proved most resistant to his message, at times outright opposing it, were those who had power and influence of some sort, including many of the devoutly religious. Given John's experiences growing up and his skepticism of dominant religious institutions, I doubt that would have surprised him in the least. According to Matthew 3:7, John rebuffed Pharisees and Sadducees who came to him for baptism. Luke 3:7, on the other hand, has John call the crowds as a whole a "brood of vipers" rather than specific groups. If Matthew is correct, we must ask why it was that John regarded these two very different religious groups so harshly that he would doubt their motives. After all, Matthew says they came to him for baptism, not to challenge or debate him.

The Sadducees were a small and very conservative group, one that had not embraced the developing collection of Scriptures but focused on torah alone. The Pharisees were on the opposite end of the spectrum, quite diverse in many ways and vibrant in their debates about how to apply the laws in torah. Both groups thought that their way of approaching what it meant to be Jewish was correct. That some of their members came to John for baptism could be interpreted as indicating that they did not in fact have everything in order. Hence John's mocking question, "who warned you to flee from the coming wrath?" They hadn't been there listening to John; they had been elsewhere listening to their own teachers. Yet someone had told them about John and his message, and they had felt the need to respond. But how deep did that response go?

John's question is much like Jesus's statement that he had not come to call the righteous but sinners (Mark 2:17). While some think the latter was meant at face value at least initially, Jesus's parables that contrast a Pharisee with a tax collector (Luke 18:9–14) and priests and Levites with a Samaritan (Luke 10:25–37) reflect the conviction that the "sinners" were aware of their problem and doing something about it, if only to express genuine remorse, seek forgiveness, and humble themselves. The purportedly righteous, on the other hand, were often confident in their righteousness, even while focused on things other than the "weightier matters" of justice and mercy (Matt. 23:23). John and Jesus both saw that the most religious of their contemporaries were not consistently the kindest, the fairest, or the most trustworthy. They were, on the other hand, typically the least receptive to having their shortcomings pointed out. John had thus not made them a focus of his activity. Even so, some of them came to him, and he couldn't help making fun of them. "My message is for sinners. Who warned you that you have something to fear from the coming wrath?" Those who were not immediately turned off by his teasing showed they had the humility and the self-awareness to question their allegiance to other groups and their teachings. Regardless of whether they thought that the right ideas and interpretations were being taught and promoted by the groups with which they were affiliated, they accepted John's message that that was not enough. To be sure, some of those Pharisees and Sadducees who came to John for baptism would have gone away sad or more likely angry after John's comments. For those who did not leave but stayed and were baptized, their experience of John's baptism would have been all the more life-changing as a result.

THE WAY

John's movement seems to have been known as "the way," taking its nickname from the language of Isaiah that John used and that others associated with him. John was the voice of one crying, "In the wilderness, prepare the way." Acts shows us that this nickname continued to be applied to the Christian movement for some time, until it eventually came to be associated less with John than with Jesus.[12] In Acts, we are introduced to another vibrant mind and spirit, a man named Apollos from Alexandria who is identified as instructed in the way of the Lord and yet simultaneously as knowing only John's baptism. The way of the Lord in this instance is the way of John, the one who called people to prepare the way of the Lord. Missing this, we fail to recognize that the two-volume Luke-Acts reveals to us a Christianity finding its own identity and wrestling with its origin as a subset of a wider movement with which it significantly overlapped.

Whether John gave his movement this name or others came up with the label, its widespread use indicates that it was felt to encapsulate something true and important about John's movement. The point of the passage in Isaiah 40, as John understood it, is that those awaiting the arrival of God need to prepare for it. In the Scriptures, God is quintessentially the one who makes the way straight and smooths the road for mortals in distress. Why then does Isaiah talk about people doing the reverse, making a straight path for God? It can mean only that the people, by straightening their own paths and doing what is right, prepare for God's arrival. The emphasis on the supreme power of God imme-

12. Joel Marcus, *John the Baptist in History and Theology* (Columbia: University of South Carolina Press, 2018), 145–47, is helpful on this topic, although he assumes a connection with Qumran.

diately afterward in Isaiah helps make the point. God's action to gather the lost sheep and bring an end to exile does not depend on humans making a literal road for God to follow. It is moral and spiritual preparation that makes a way for God to arrive in a manner that benefits the people. The ancient prophets regularly warned against hoping for God's arrival without being prepared.

Jesus echoed the way John spoke, telling how the arrival of the judgment that was coming would catch off guard those who did not dedicate themselves to constant vigilance (Luke 12:40, 46 // Matt. 24:44, 50). Here we see how the strands in the infancy story Luke tells about John and the strands in the message John proclaimed come together. God did indeed have a special relationship with the children of Abraham. The specialness of the relationship and God's commitment to it had never been the problem. It was the people who had turned their backs on God and the way of God. God was faithful to the descendants of Abraham, which is precisely why God had put up with their sins and waywardness for so long. That did not get them off the hook when God showed up in strength and power to act.

God's faithfulness was why he had sent John and was giving them one more chance. John's message was stern and serious but not unhopeful.[13] He did not walk around like Jonah predicting Nineveh's downfall while giving no indication that fate might be avoided and how. In a manner that resonates in a very striking way with John's words, Isaiah 43 tells the people not to fear passing through waters and rivers, or even through fire. Those who seek first the kingdom of God and the justice associated with it do not need to fear, except in the positive sense of having the overwhelming sense of awe appropriate in relation to the incomparable God. The section of Isaiah we have been talking about continues with an emphasis on God gathering the people from far and wide. God himself will make a way in the wilderness (43:19). What can this

13. See the helpful discussion in Knut Backhaus, "Echoes from the Wilderness: The Historical John the Baptist," in Handbook for the Study of the Historical Jesus, ed. Tom Holmén and Stanley E. Porter (Leiden: Brill, 2011), 2:1767. He writes, "The threshing floor—the land and people of Israel may be associated—will be cleansed but not destroyed. The metaphorical framework of John's preaching clearly indicates both the dominant position of the judgment motif and the hopeful prospect that those who repent—i.e. who submit to John's baptism and adjust their lives to its conditions—would be spared." This is also relevant to the question of whether John expected an end of history or a major turning point within history, which we go on to explore.

mean in light of the earlier statement, except that God has sent John to prepare the people and the way? God does not simply tell the people to prepare but works through his prophet to help them do so. These chapters in Isaiah go on to reassure Jacob's descendants and yet at the same time also insist that God has been wearied by their sin. God will forgive and redeem, and ultimately every knee will bow and every tongue acknowledge the supremacy and power of God. But some will do so with joy and others with shame.

John's call to the nation emphasizes that the kingdom of God will arrive and will be a reason for unprecedented joy for those who have repented and changed their ways in preparation. Despite not having anything more than hints of what John's sermons and teaching must have been like, it is not difficult to piece together the gist of what these might have been like from what we are told about John's emphases and about the texts he gravitated toward.

John's Apostles

John had apostles. The English word "apostle" is a transliteration of a Greek word meaning one who is sent—an emissary, ambassador, agent, or representative. We saw in the case of Jesus's temple action that he performed it while part of John's movement. Whether Jesus had set himself apart early and quickly, or rose through the ranks of John's followers, we get a sense that he was not simply a disciple of John's but a leader in John's movement. Many people came to John for baptism, a smaller number became his disciples and studied with him, and an even smaller number were his inner circle, his "graduate assistants" we might say, who could be involved in teaching his courses (to continue the analogy). Those were the people that John would send out to proclaim his message and baptize in other places. Jesus was among them, and we get the sense that he may have become John's leading disciple, his assistant and go-to person to deliver his message and undertake symbolic actions that contributed to the spread of his message and his baptismal practice. Sources outside the New Testament suggest that others may have played a similar role to that which Jesus played in the movement but perhaps in different areas.[14]

14. In addition to Simon and Dositheus in Samaria, we may note the Mandaean Book of John, which mentions several names of individuals who represent a core of John's follow-

In the Gospel of Mark, it is Jesus's sending out of emissaries to proclaim the kingdom that draws Jesus to Herod's attention (Mark 6:7–16). Herod's reaction is to think Jesus is John returned from the dead. This clues us in that Jesus's activities resembled those of John, which is not surprising since at that stage, Jesus was the emerging leader of John's continuing movement. Just as the action of Jesus in the temple and other activities by John's emissaries drew the attention of authorities to John and his movement, the same happened in the case of Jesus, who followed John's pattern, which helpfully allows us to fill in information about John's approach to spreading his message. However much or little John moved around, we are told that crowds flocked to him where he was to be found, as they later would to Jesus. It is easy for a modern reader of these ancient stories not to consider how difficult it was to accomplish something like that in ancient times. Even with today's high-tech telecommunications, one can struggle to generate attendance at a meeting or event. John did not even have posters and flyers, much less TV commercials or an Instagram account. How did he generate so much attention and excitement? By sending out some of his earliest and best-trained disciples to baptize and teach as well as heal people and carry out exorcisms.

The way of God that John and his representatives proclaimed was facilitated by John's way with words. In just the few sayings attributed to him in the New Testament, we find puns and plays on words, striking imagery, and evocative metaphors. Mandaean sources agree with the New Testament on this point, just as they agree in depicting John as teaching practical righteousness with a strong focus on social and economic justice. Describing how John went about proclaiming his message and where he found his audience, we did not stop to consider the fact that, particularly in the early days of his efforts, few if any would have immediately embraced what John was saying. They would have carried on their way toward Jerusalem. John's clever turns of phrase would have stayed with them, however, and some would have stopped to listen and talk for longer on their return journey. As John's fame grew, he eventually reached the

---

ers. While the names may not be historical, the impression of such a core, which includes leaders in their own right like Meryey (Mary), may nonetheless reflect the historical reality. A Syriac author refers to Mandaeans as Dositheans, which is striking and may reflect an ongoing awareness that gnostics with a focus of John the Baptist emerged via that route. Samaritan evidence, on the other hand, suggests that not all Dositheans were or became gnostics, and early church sources connect the origins of Gnosticism with Simon.

point that people sought him out and welcomed his envoys who showed up in their towns and villages. Some of those envoys, as we see from the famous example of Jesus, were gifted in much the same way as John was in their own right, telling memorable parables and pithy sayings that were impossible to forget.

Conclusion

As we have emphasized throughout this book, the wilderness was important to John for many reasons, but seeking to be a hermit who removed himself from society was not one of them. For John, as for Moses and Elijah in the scriptural stories, the wilderness was not a place where prophets isolated themselves indefinitely but a place where they encountered God and found new strength and purpose for their activity within society. When Jesus withdrew to solitary places for periods of time, thereafter to return to his mission, he was following John's example. When they did so, neither went all that far from major thoroughfares, and both returned from wherever they went to continue their mission of seeking the lost sheep of Israel. John and his followers, after taking time away to commune with God and discuss and learn from one another, returned to the literal way in order to seek those who had lost their metaphorical way. John's diverse entourage was objectionable to many, as much to Jews as to Samaritans. That aspect of John's message would be taken in a radical direction by Paul and some other Christians, while many of John's followers would, after his death, return to their native places and focus on their own people. John's vision inspired many others who would take things in directions that differed at least somewhat from his own, while building on the foundation he had laid. John got the attention he did from authorities because he was connected, not primarily by family ties (although those are always part of the picture in some way) but because he had a powerful vision and was a gifted speaker who could inspire people.

This chapter has hopefully conveyed a sense of both how successful John was and how John was successful. The question the successful inevitably face is, What next? This was not for John a question of what to do for an encore, or of how to sustain his popularity as though that were an end in itself. Generation after generation, there had been at least some who seemed willing to hearken to the voice of a prophet. It didn't last. Whether that mattered for

John in the same way it had for others before him depends on whether you think he expected that he was living at the end of history. Some of what he said certainly sounds like that was his vision. Other things he said, however, suggest that what he saw on the horizon was a decisive moment of judgment within history, a key turning point rather than its end. The next chapter will clarify whether it was one or the other, or both. Either way, one thing was clear. What he had said and done thus far had set the stage for something monumental. Before the decisive moment arrived, however, something more was needed—or rather someone.

Someone Is Coming

This chapter brings us to the topic that provides the title for this life of John: his role as Christmaker. As a result of Christian literature about him, John the Baptist is most famous as the precursor of Jesus. Most historians correctly insist that John did not think of himself as Jesus's forerunner. Even when he spoke of another who would come after him, it was not as though he had Jesus specifically in mind. While one could imagine John being vague so as not to put his successor unnecessarily in harm's way before the time was right, it is much more likely that John saw his prediction of a stronger one to emerge from among his followers as an invitation rather than a reference to someone already identified. Some have doubted that John spoke of a coming one, or have thought that he saw himself as a precursor to the arrival of a stronger one who was none other than God himself. Most historians conclude that he spoke of another human figure. The reasoning is simple. First, if Christians had invented John's predictions, they would have made them match who Jesus actually turned out to be, what he was like. When the Gospel of John depicts Jesus not as the stronger one but the Lamb of God, we can detect the rewriting that has taken place compared to what John says in the earlier gospels. Second, the prediction reveals something that Christian sources otherwise avoid saying. Across the gospel tradition, John speaks of "one who comes after me" who will be revealed to be stronger than he. That language of coming after is familiar to readers of the New Testament as the terminology for discipleship. It was about one of his followers that John spoke thus. Finally, the image of not being worthy to carry, or not fit to untie, the sandals of the coming one is an expression of humility if it referred to one of his disciples, while it is downright farcical if John was talking about God.

Before Jesus sought to occupy the role of John's predicted figure, John made the prediction. Our focus here is on making clear what John actually said, what he expected and hoped for. Of course, to the extent that Jesus stepped into that role, and to the extent that his later followers had to explain why Jesus did not quite match what John's other followers expected, it helps us understand what John meant as we survey the efforts to reinterpret John's role as precursor specifically to Jesus. Moreover, by speaking of another stronger than he, John helps us to understand not just his vision for the future but his own self-understanding. People had been wondering whether John might be the Messiah, according to Luke 3:15–18. Luke makes John's talk of a coming one his answer to such speculation. Yet John's prediction did not exclude the possibility of a messianic understanding of himself as well. To understand that, we must consider what "Messiah" meant in John's time, what it would have meant for people to ponder whether John was that figure.

Two Messiahs

"Messiah" (from Hebrew) and "Christ" (from Greek) are simply ways of saying "anointed." The term could be used in reference to two major roles in ancient Israel, the king and the high priest, whose ceremonies of installation in that office included oil being poured or smeared on them. Both the kingship and the high priesthood were, in John's time, no longer in the hands of those whom most Jews considered to be their rightful holders: the descendants of Aaron via Zadok for the high priesthood and the descendants of David for the kingship. While not everyone minded (the Hasmonean rulers happily accepted both titles despite being from neither of the appropriate lineages), some certainly did hope for the restoration of both institutions to the dynasties to which, according to the Scriptures, they belonged. Hence the existence in this time of messianic expectations, which were by no means universal or all the same.

It has been suggested that John understood himself as the priestly messiah, with his stronger one who is to come a royal figure. If so, John was a truly subversive claimant to that role. Some ancient Christian stories about John's father make him the high priest, perhaps reflecting the view among John's followers

that John was the fulfillment of these messianic hopes and had the genealogy necessary to fit what was expected. If John thought of himself in those
terms at all, he was not claiming to fit expectations but was radically redefining
them—in which case, it is much less surprising that Jesus and his followers did
likewise with respect to his status as Davidic Messiah. Some would eventually
come to view John as the only messianic figure, one who would rule and lead
as well as mediate God's message and God's forgiveness, much as Moses had.
Prophet, priest, and king all rolled into one. When Christians developed their
all-encompassing, multifaceted vision of Jesus as the fulfillment of everything
people were hoping for and more, they were not the first to do so. Nor, as we
have seen, was John. One could be priest and prophet, or king and priest, or
various other configurations. In some cases, claiming those roles for oneself
necessarily involved reinterpreting or ignoring the lineages of descent that
were felt necessary if one were to legitimately hold the title in question. John
was of priestly descent but not high priestly (although some later claimed
that). As a priest and a Nazirite who was prevented from offering sacrifices in
the temple, he seems not to have seen himself as fulfilling the hopes for restoration of the high priesthood to the line of Aaron and his descendant Zadok,
the hope in particular among the Essenes. John was offering something new,
albeit with precedents in the Scriptures and the history of Israel.

One figure who loomed large in John's mind by virtue of his lifelong Nazirite status was Samuel, the prophet who was a Nazirite yet who also played
a priestly role. Moreover, Samuel was the prophet who anointed David to be
king (1 Sam. 16:13). Thus as a new Samuel, John might still have viewed himself
as relating to a stronger one who would not be his superior (the king was to
be subordinate to the voice of God through a prophet), but stronger (just as
a king would act with military force in a way that prophets as a rule did not).
Yet despite the echoes of Samuel in the infancy story, John's choice of figure
to emulate from Israel's history was not Samuel but Elijah.

It is not impossible that Elijah himself was a Nazirite, a "hairy man," which
perhaps refers to his unkempt hair, even as it was later interpreted as a reference to his haircloth clothing.[1] Elijah was succeeded by Elisha, his disciple
who did act as a stronger one in relation to him, arranging the anointing
of Jehu to overthrow the dynasty of Omri and eliminate the worship of

---

1. Note as well how Amos 2:11–12 parallels Nazirites and prophets.

Baal (2 Kings 9–10). While the response of Jesus to John's question about whether he was the coming one, depicted in Matthew and Luke, echoes particularly strongly with Isaiah 35:5–8 (a passage that also connects with John's beloved theme of the way in the wilderness), there are also overtones of Elisha there and elsewhere. He helped the poor (2 Kings 4:1–7), raised the dead (2 Kings 4:34; 13:21), healed a leper (2 Kings 5:14), and restored vision after causing blindness (2 Kings 6:18–20). Note as well the echoes of 2 Kings 4:43–44 in the stories about Jesus multiplying food.[2] John's prediction of a stronger one could envisage a prophetic disciple who, unlike Elijah and unlike John, would act to bring about the end of Herodian reign, purge the unrepentant wicked from among the people, and bring about the rule of all Israel by someone who would practice justice and righteousness.[3] The imagery does not imply that the stronger one will be the one to so rule, although neither does it exclude the possibility. Ultimately, even if the typology of Elijah and Elisha was foremost in John's mind, we should not impose any of these types onto John's vision too rigidly. They all likely inspired him but none constrained him. The coming one would be something new just as he, John himself, was something new.

John's message to Jesus asking whether he is the coming one (Matt. 11:3 // Luke 7:19) has often been treated as an indication of doubt on John's part. We get this mistaken impression because the developing gospel tradition came to depict John as recognizing who Jesus was from the outset. Matthew 3:14–15 is an addition by that gospel's author not found in any other in the New Testament. Our earliest sources indicate that John predicted that one would arise from among his followers without specifying who or necessarily knowing himself. John's question is thus best understood as both an invitation and a request for information. Jesus had regrouped John's followers, but that didn't mean Jesus saw himself as the coming one. Taking John's place leading the group, he might still be looking forward to someone else still to come as John had.

2. See further Vernon K. Robbins, *Who Do People Say I Am? Rewriting Gospel in Emerging Christianity* (Grand Rapids: Eerdmans, 2013), 17–19; Joel Marcus, *John the Baptist in History and Theology* (Columbia: University of South Carolina Press, 2018), 87–89.

3. See Daniel W. McManigal, *A Baptism of Judgment in the Fire of the Holy Spirit: John's Eschatological Proclamation in Matthew 3*, Library of New Testament Studies (London: Bloomsbury, 2019), 93–102, on John and Jesus as prophets in the Gospel of Matthew.

The way Jesus spoke of the Son of Man who would come may have made things especially ambiguous. While the Gospels give us only an extremely succinct summation of John's forward-looking expectations, Jesus's Son of Man sayings help to fill in the picture. In Aramaic, "Son of Man" simply means "person," and when Jesus used it in the emphatic form, it meant "the person" or "the one." To which person, one, or someone was Jesus referring when he coupled the expression "Son of Man" with the verb "to come"? The "one who is to come" about whom John spoke. The church, in remembering Jesus speaking about the coming Son of Man, and identifying Jesus as that very figure, was saying that Jesus would eventually fulfill the role of the stronger one about whom John spoke. First, however, he had to suffer even as his mentor John had suffered. It was only by that route, by humbling oneself, that one could hope to be exalted by God in the kingdom that was coming.

Although we will focus on it more in the next chapter, we need to mention the death of John here because that event had an enormous impact on Jesus. We saw in an earlier chapter that Jesus's action in the temple may have been the direct trigger leading Antipas to arrest and execute John. Ultimately this moment represented a turning point for him and may have led him to begin to reinterpret the role of the coming one in ways that his later followers would need to take further still. Jesus still believed he was the one whom John said would come, but that would not come about through his action or that of his supporters. His path would be like that of John himself, leading to arrest and suffering. Only if he embraced John's path would God elevate him to the role of power and judgment ascribed to the coming one. Ironically, it was Jesus being too much like John, rather than Jesus having departed from his teaching, that caused numerous followers of John to reject Jesus. They understood John to have predicted a coming one who would be different from him in strength and the exercise thereof. In other words, they expected someone who would be victorious and in the process vindicate the message and prediction of John, whose execution otherwise would represent defeat. When Jesus embraced a path of suffering as the necessary prelude to his acting in strength to judge, it was not inherently incompatible with him being John's stronger one. But once Jesus was crucified, many of John's followers who had "hoped that he was the one to redeem Israel" (Luke 24:21) were disappointed. They found unconvincing the claims of Jesus's supporters that he had been vindicated beyond death and would eventually do what John predicted.

THE KINGDOMS OF GOD AND OF THIS WORLD

Many view the context of the Roman Empire as the most crucial element of background to the apocalypticism of Jesus, John, and others of their contemporaries. Yet Rome was just the latest in a long line of empires within whose borders the land of Israel found itself. At no point in its history had there not been a more powerful neighbor, whether near or distant, with which the ruler of the people had had to negotiate. Royal marriages were a key part of local alliances. In Herod Antipas's case, marriage to the daughter of the Arabian king Aretas sought to turn this mutual ally of Rome yet onetime enemy of his father into a friend.[4] Like many other members of his family, Antipas was educated in Rome.[5] At one point, Josephus indicates that his mother was Malthace, a Samaritan, although other statements seem to contradict this.[6] Either way, the Herodian dynasty included lineages and intermarriages from a range of peoples and territories in the region, Israelites (Jews and Samaritans) as well as Idumeans (Edomites) and Nabataeans (Arabians).

This sort of multiculturalism was typical of the time and not that uncommon in any era, especially in monarchies. The biblical stories about the kingdoms of Israel and Judah do not always indicate this, but the archaeological record does. None of this was, as far as we can tell, a problem for John. He criticized Antipas for divorcing his Nabataean wife, not for marrying her. The depiction of first-century Jews as extremely xenophobic is a result of the desire of Christians to have Jesus stand out positively against the uniformly negative backdrop of his time. There certainly were nationalists in that era, as in all others, but their outlook was not the only one. It is no surprise that John and Jesus would resemble one another in this regard. Both were proud of their Jewish

4. Bruce Chilton, *The Herods: Murder, Politics, and the Art of Succession* (Minneapolis: Fortress, 2021), 151–52, https://doi.org/10.2307/j.ctv1khdnxr.

5. On Antipas's education, see Jonathan Marshall, *Jesus, Patrons, and Benefactors: Roman Palestine and the Gospel of Luke* (Tübingen: Mohr Siebeck, 2009), 137.

6. For Malthace as Antipas's mother, see *Jewish War* 1.562 and *Jewish Antiquities* 17.20–21. For the other statements that call this information into question, see Daniel R. Schwartz, "Malthace, Archelaus, and Herod Antipas: Between Genealogy and Typology," in *Sources and Interpretation in Ancient Judaism: Studies for Tal Ilan at Sixty*, ed. Meron Piotrkowski, Geoffrey Herman, and Saskia Doenitz (Leiden: Brill, 2018), 32–40, https://doi.org/10.1163/9789004366985.

heritage and sought to be faithful to the God of their ancestors. Neither was characterized by animosity toward anyone who wasn't Jewish, and neither of them was unusual in their time because of this.

The eras in which the kingdoms of Judah and Israel had the greatest relative independence did not correspond to the times of greatest righteousness. If anything, one might detect an inverse correlation. It is thus not surprising that John did not focus on themes of liberation from imperial rule that other apocalyptic preachers were prone to. The native Jewish leaders of recent memory, whether Hasmoneans or Herodians, were all part of the problem rather than the solution. None led the nation toward doing what is right. None exemplified justice on a national level in such a way as might have inspired the local practice of justice, nor did they make laws that fostered that. To hope for national restoration, led by a high priest and a king from the correct lineages, was not necessarily inappropriate, but it was foolhardy and misguided to seek such things as ends in themselves. Those things would come about only in response to the people keeping covenant with their God. As Jesus would later echo, John called the people to seek first the kingdom of God and its justice, with anything else a blessing God might bestow on those who prioritize submission and obedience to what God has commanded.

This is not to suggest that John's message was apolitical. The notion that you could criticize a ruler's behavior but still be a loyal citizen was as foreign to John's time as the notion of separation of church and state.[7] Speaking about God's kingdom could not but have implications for the kingdoms of this world in general, and kingdoms of Israel and Judah whether real or imagined. John criticized Antipas and gathered crowds that hung on his every word. That was a dangerous combination, and it is entirely predictable that John was arrested and executed. We might then ask why John considered it important and worthwhile to publicly criticize the tetrarch when he must surely have known what would follow. The answer is presumably that John saw what was wrong in the society exemplified in Herod Antipas's divorce and remarriage. His action was entirely self-serving, the exact opposite of what is at the heart of every moral teaching attributed to John the Baptist. Herod Antipas cared not about the

---

7. As Chilton, *Herods*, 157, writes, "An assertion that his marriage was illegitimate amounted to delegitimating Antipas's rule in terms of Judaism, and he did not shrink from striking back against John."

well-being of his first wife or any contract with her, or about the people who would be impacted if (as turned out to be the case) relations among the Herodians as well as between Antipas and Aretas of Arabia soured. John's criticism of Herod for divorcing his first wife and marrying Herodias may have had as much to do with the warfare with Arabia that was sure to result as with the illegality of marrying a brother's wife. If John ignored Antipas's behavior while calling out others, it would only have been out of a desire for self-preservation, and John could scarcely call others to sacrifice their own well-being for the sake of others while not doing that himself.

Nothing about John or his baptism would have led of necessity to his prediction of a stronger one who is to come. It thus makes sense to suggest that an awareness that he would soon be apprehended was the immediate trigger for him to say that one of his disciples would prove to be stronger than he. The wording is naturally understood as a response to the threat against him with a threat of his own. "You think that you can get rid of me and stop what I have begun? There's a follower of mine, you don't know which one, who is stronger than I, as you'll see. If you think I have caused trouble, you haven't seen anything yet." The Gospels differ on whether John spoke of carrying or untying the sandals of the one of whom John spoke, and whether he said he was unworthy or not fit for the task. It is thus hard to know whether John said he wasn't worthy even to be the slave of that individual, or that his strength was such that John, himself a person of strength, would not be in sufficient shape even to untie the thong of his sandal. Either way, the point was clear. Get rid of John, and they'll have a worse problem on their hands. I doubt that John expected Antipas to be put off by his counterthreat and back down.[8] John's statement was more likely aimed at his followers: get ready for what is to come, and at least one of you get ready to lead the movement and take things to the next level. One of the historical questions related to John the Baptist that has attracted particular attention over the years is whether John had someone in particular in mind. The way things unfolded suggests that if he did, he never made that explicit. Jesus appears to have been the first of John's followers to

8. Although we cannot rely too heavily on the information in the Gospel of Luke about when John was born, the impression it gives that John and Antipas were roughly the same age is worth mentioning as part of the picture of their conflict. A threat from a peer is often more worrying than one from someone significantly older or younger.

step into the role and seek to regroup John's followers after his arrest, but he would not be the last.

HEAVENLY COUNTERPARTS

We spoke earlier in the book about the fact that John must certainly have baptized himself before asking others to do so. The conviction that he was authorized to proclaim this new means of forgiveness tells us that when he immersed himself, he had a profoundly life-altering experience as a result, one that convinced him his mission must be to invite others to have the same experience he did.[9] It might have been helpful to present this important background to John's public activity earlier in the book. The reason for waiting until now is that it is only in the context of John's prediction of the coming one, and the things said about Jesus and the Son of Man, that we can get a full sense of what his experience was, in light of what others experienced who underwent his baptism. Have you ever noticed the way the New Testament discusses whether John was Elijah? Some of those writings are careful to emphasize that he was not Elijah himself returned but one who came "in the spirit and power of Elijah" (Luke 1:17). When Jesus asks who people say that he is, the answer is of a similar sort. "John the Baptist; and others, Elijah; and still others, one of the prophets" (Mark 8:27–28; see also 6:14–16). Do you see the pattern? Both John and Jesus were viewed as in some sense embodying the presence of key figures from the past. But in what sense?

The story of Jesus's baptism, as told by Christians, could convey the impression that Jesus was the only one to have a spiritual experience in connection with John's baptism. That does not appear to be the point initially, as nothing is said to that effect in our earliest sources. Indeed, they make clear that at least one person (Jesus) had an experience of receiving the Spirit when undergoing John's baptism. Whatever John meant when he said that the coming one would immerse people in fire, spirit, or both, it clearly did not preclude that John himself could be viewed as full of the Holy Spirit (Luke 1:15) and that

9. For the wider background and the primary texts that provide evidence for it, see Andrei A. Orlov, *The Greatest Mirror: Heavenly Counterparts in the Jewish Pseudepigrapha* (Albany: State University of New York Press, 2017), 92, 115, 136.

Jesus could experience the Spirit when he was baptized (Mark 1:8; Matt. 3:11; Luke 3:16). In Acts 8:10, Simon (who is identified as one of John's disciples in other sources, as we mentioned previously) is said to in some sense be a divine power that is called "Great." The depiction of him offering money to be able to bestow God's Spirit on others (Acts 8:18–19), like the depiction of others among John's disciples as not even having heard there is a Holy Spirit (Acts 19:1–6), is an attempt to denigrate that movement as inadequate while emphasizing the need even for those who underwent John's baptism to be rebaptized and join the emerging Christian movement. Taken together, we get a sense that John's baptism was indeed, for some people at least, an occasion for a spiritual rebirth of some sort.

Acts 12:15 provides a reference to a widely held viewpoint in that time that allows us to pull these threads together. Each individual was thought to have a celestial counterpart, and thus when someone that seemed to be Peter, yet couldn't possibly be, appeared at the door, the suggestion was made that it was his angel.[10] If everyone had angelic doubles, and if Elisha could have received a double portion of Elijah's spirit (2 Kings 2:9, 15), then it was possible not merely to have an experience of one's own celestial counterpart but to be filled with the presence and power of the heavenly counterpart of one of the great heroes of the past. Thus John could be the conduit for the spirit and power of Elijah, and Jesus might do the same in relation to John the Baptist, or Elijah, or one of the other prophets.

The Parables of Enoch speak of a messianic figure whom Enoch views in heaven (and who is referred to as "that human figure" using the expression "that Son of Man"). While 1 Enoch 71.14 may or may not have intended to identify Enoch himself as that Son of Man, later Jewish tradition did so.[11] Even-

10. It was disappointing to see N. T. Wright, in an article supposedly aimed at correcting widespread misperceptions of ancient Christian views of the afterlife, treat this story as though it were about seeing Peter's *ghost* (Tish Harrison Warren, "Did Jesus Really Rise from the Dead?," *New York Times*, April 9, 2023, https://www.nytimes.com/2023/04/09/opinion/jesus-rise-from-the-dead-easter.html). Contrary to a view that is widespread in some circles, the early Christians did not believe that the spirits of the dead were or became angels. Jesus himself said that in the resurrection (but not as disembodied spirits), the resurrected would be like angels (Matt. 22:30).

11. On the Son of Man as Jesus's heavenly counterpart, see Dale C. Allison, *Constructing Jesus: Memory, Imagination, and History* (Grand Rapids: Baker, 2010), 294–303.

tually, Enoch is identified as God's chief celestial assistant, called Metatron. As one who ascended to heaven and united with or was transformed into that celestial figure, he could now guide others who sought to experience a mystical heavenly journey. It is just possible that some of the later literary works about Enoch and Metatron may have been responses to the ideas that John shared with his followers. Alternatively, they may simply have been expressions of a shared framework of mysticism. Either way, the sources we have considered thus far give us a sense of the mystical aspect of John's baptism.

Presumably when John first underwent it himself, on his own, as yet not elaborated into a rite that he would proclaim to others, he both felt something and saw something. John could have seen himself connected with his own individual angelic counterpart, or with that of some other figure. The way that he styled himself after Elijah suggests that as he came up from the water with a feeling that something had changed inside him, he also caught a glimpse of his image in the water and somehow saw it as that of Elijah. Later, he would teach his followers to seek their own life-changing experience of the same sort. Beyond the New Testament, we find that still others from John's circle, and those who became part of it after his death, continued this aspect of his life and teaching.

Sign Prophets

The Jewish historian Flavius Josephus mentions not only John and Jesus but a series of other similar figures who came along later. Modern scholars have long made a habit of discussing them when trying to contextualize John and Jesus. They are frequently grouped together under the heading "sign prophets," and that is the reason for this section bearing the same title. What needs to be recognized is that we need not only to compare these figures to John but to *connect* them to John. When Martin Luther King Jr. began utilizing in the United States the same methods that Mohandas Gandhi had put to such effective use in India, a historian who did not have evidence of deliberate emulation would still be justified in positing influence. In the same way, when figure after figure appears on the scene among the Jews and Samaritans doing things similar to John and Jesus, we must posit influence, deliberate emulation, or both.

The earliest of the individuals mentioned by Josephus is, interestingly, a Samaritan who appeared in AD 36 (*Jewish Antiquities* 18.4.1) and led a group to

Mount Gerizim, their place of worship, claiming that when they did so, sacred vessels hidden there by Moses would be revealed. Pontius Pilate sent troops and killed many of the group, including the leader. About a decade later, in AD 46, an individual called Theudas, whose name likely meant "flowing with water," called people with him to the Jordan, saying he would divide it, as Elijah and then Elisha had done (*Jewish Antiquities* 20.5.1). The Roman procurator Fadus sent troops, killed many of the group, and after apprehending Theudas had him beheaded, just as John had been. Fast-forward another decade, and we find several individuals during the period while Felix was in charge, including one who led a group into the wilderness in expectation of signs, and another who came from Egypt, claimed to be a prophet, and led a group to the Mount of Olives saying that the walls of Jerusalem would fall at his command. A couple of others could be mentioned, but these will suffice as the figures about whom we are provided with the most details.[12]

When we see how many similarities and points of connection with John (and Jesus, and Simon Magus) there are, only one conclusion is justified. These are not coincidentally similar expressions of some prevailing spirit of the age but figures associated with John's movement who believed that they were destined to be the stronger one of whom John spoke. The earliest of them may have had a direct connection with John. Those who came later may have arisen from the next generation of the movement. After Jesus seemed for all intents and purposes to have failed to do the things expected of the coming one, others in John's movement considered that perhaps they were the one to play that role. It is likely that, when the New Testament authors speak of many who will come saying "I am he" and of figures who say "he is in the wilderness," they are warning about such figures, insisting that Jesus will be shown to be the one after all, and it is important to remain true to him (Mark 13:6; Matt. 24:26). Taken together, we get a sense of what the prediction of John most likely had in view, to have inspired these other figures.

John must have spoken of a figure who would perform a powerful sign, without specifying which one. In the case of Jesus, it was predicting the temple would be destroyed and rebuilt, while others predicted other signs would

12. See further on these figures, P. W. Barnett, "The Jewish Sign Prophets—A.D. 40–70: Their Intentions and Origin," *New Testament Studies* 27 (1981): 679, https://doi.org/10.1017/S0028688500007165.

accompany them, as we have just listed from Josephus. Each individual, their location, and their sign connected them in some way with a key figure from the biblical tradition, whether Elisha or Joshua or Moses. All of them, in other words, reflect John's fostering, at least among his inner circle of followers, of a mystical experience of identification with a heroic figure from the past and the miracle(s) they accomplished.

These figures seem noticeably different from the many others whom Josephus lists who carried weapons and engaged in acts of violence. Yet he lists them all together and views them all as evidence of the troubled character of these decades. He acknowledged that such individuals and their followers had "purer hands" than those who committed murder but nonetheless considered them culpable for their contribution to the unrest.[13] It is striking that Josephus does not criticize John the Baptist, or Jesus, in the same manner, perhaps for the simple reason that neither brought a group to a specific place to await a miracle that would lead to some sort of deliverance. The evidence we have points to John the Baptist having taught nonviolence. The Mandaeans and the earliest Christians espoused this stance, presumably indicating that this shared element goes back to John. Yet nonviolent religious movements and violent revolutionary ones may reinforce one another as the former generate and keep alive an expectation that the moment for change has arrived, and the latter seek to make it happen. Indeed, to the extent that Elisha may have been John's pattern for the stronger one, we must remember that Elisha actively brought about regime change that included, in the case of Jehu, extremely violent overthrow of the previous dynasty and elimination of all of its family members and all the religious leaders aligned with it. There was nothing inherently outlandish in associating the two, and there would have been nothing incongruous if individuals in John's movement who did not take up arms incited those who did.

We do not have any evidence that John was directly involved in fomenting violence. My own inclination is to see both him and Jesus as expecting God to work only through those who humbled themselves and were willing to suffer for doing what is right, while loving their enemies rather than taking up arms against them. I am convinced that the evidence supports this interpretation. However,

13. See further on this topic, Nathan C. Johnson, "Early Jewish Sign Prophets," in *Critical Dictionary of Apocalyptic and Millenarian Movements*, ed. James Crossley and Alastair Lockhart, December 8, 2021, https://www.cdamm.org/articles/early-jewish-sign-prophets.

knowing the history of prophetic involvement in violent regime change, and knowing there can be political parties and paramilitary organizations that are entangled while seeking to maintain at least some appearance of being distinct, I cannot rule out the possibility that John saw where his prediction and his language would lead and did not shy away from it. I am also aware that I bring assumptions about Jesus with me, and a desire to view him in a particular way, that cannot but influence my thinking about his mentor John. Nonetheless, given how allegiance to revolutionaries tends to die when they do, the persistence of the followers of John and of Jesus beyond their deaths suggests to me that they were clearly not figures of that sort, even if we must add that neither are they separable from the political events and activities of their era.

When we recognize that so many individuals and events described by Josephus in his account of this period owed a debt of influence to John the Baptist, whether directly or indirectly, it allows us to draw an important conclusion as a corollary. The Jewish war against Rome that resulted in the destruction of Jerusalem and its temple in AD 70 might not have unfolded as it did had there been no John the Baptist. The combined evidence of the New Testament and Josephus, especially once we trace all the relevant connections, shows that there was no other figure in that era who had a greater impact. On the one hand, many of those who took up arms to try to change things (or simply to seize power for themselves), at the very least, took advantage of the fervor generated by John and his movement. On the other hand, the influence of John's teachings on subjects like repentance, humility, and nonviolence may have prevented the war from being even more calamitous than it was. John's message that the time had come to do without the temple and experience God's forgiveness anywhere and everywhere also undoubtedly contributed to how widespread that view came to be in Judaism thereafter, with the result that relatively few have sought to rebuild the temple since its destruction. The fact that other strands of Judaism did not require John's baptismal rite does not lessen the importance of his influence on the spirit of his age. The key figures in any age of history are important in their influence even on those who define themselves negatively in relation to them, or who selectively take up one of their key emphases while jettisoning others. When, in our final chapter, we trace all these connections further still across the centuries, we will find the conclusion to be undeniable that John was one of the most influential people who ever lived, as far as the history of religion is concerned.

MORE THAN A PROPHET

It has been rare for anyone to speculate on, much less draw evidenced historical conclusions about, the mystical and experiential side of John's life. Yet merely the fact that so many people regarded him as a prophet ought to have been enough to lead us to deduce that this *must* have been part of his life. A biographer, writing about any mystic, never has access to their inner life. Their writings, if they left any behind, will as often as not be replete with indications that they did not find words adequate to express what they experienced. Yet by studying many such figures, and being open to exploring such experiences, a historian can offer something that, however inadequately, at least provides a glimpse of this facet of the life of the mystic, the seer, the prophet, the poet. That last entry on the list may surprise some, but most of the prophets of ancient Israel were poets, and there isn't as enormous a gulf between artistic and religious inspiration as some have wished to claim, often out of an interest in distinguishing their inspired Scriptures or inspired leaders from others. John, as we have already observed, was this kind of figure, who had a message to proclaim and a gift for expressing it memorably, feeling strongly that his own indignation at the injustice and accompanying worship of his contemporaries was mirrored in God's own abhorrence.

The accusation that John "has a demon" (Matt. 11:18) was probably not only due to the course of life that he pursued in defiance of his priestly ancestry. It also reflects the perception that he was a conduit for spiritual power, a practitioner and promoter of spiritual experiences that not everyone had. The question of whether an individual was labeled as a prophet or as demon possessed in ancient times depended largely on whether the one doing the labeling liked what they had to say. Many acclaimed John as a prophet, the vast majority of them people who had no personal experience of the kind of mystical exploration John and some of his followers pursued. Just as many came to Jesus and sought healing and exorcism without becoming exorcists themselves, while some of his followers learned what Jesus did and became practitioners, most who recognized John as a spokesperson for God did so precisely because they perceived a power to be at work in him that was not like anything they themselves had experienced. This is in keeping with the prophetic tradition as we find it exemplified in the writings of the Jewish Scriptures, including in the particularly relevant cases of Elijah and Elisha. Second Kings 2:15 and 9:1 mention the "sons of the prophets," which suggests the existence of something that might be called a "school of the prophets." Elisha had been Elijah's disciple, and Elisha in turn had disciples and emissaries. John's movement and its offshoots appear to have been very similar.

Christians have had a tendency to insist that Jesus is more than a prophet. Jesus himself felt the same instinct in relation to his mentor John (Matt. 11:9 // Luke 7:26). That is an honor that it is possible for both to share. Christians also tend to say that Jesus was the greatest person who ever lived. At this point, Jesus himself begs to differ. Jesus stated in no uncertain terms that John the Baptist was the greatest human being who ever lived, without exception. "Among those born of women no one is greater than John" (Luke 7:28; see also Matt. 11:11). The statement that follows immediately after in these gospels ("yet the least in the kingdom of God is greater than he") should not be understood as revoking the compliment Jesus had just paid him. Those who enter the kingdom of God are a subset of those born of women; that is to say, they are human beings, and so one cannot set the two in opposition the way many Christian interpreters of the Gospels do. The meaning must be something else, and there are two possibilities. One is that Jesus was saying that those who see the kingdom of God dawn in all its fullness have an advantage that John did not, since he died before that. It would be like someone saying that no one was greater than Moses, and yet the least of those who entered the promised land was greater than he. That would not mean they were more significant prophets or mediators of covenants, or even simply better human beings. It would just be a way of emphasizing that they had a privilege that Moses missed out on. The other possibility is that Jesus is saying that the least person in the kingdom of God, when it fully dawns, will be greater then than John, the greatest human being ever, is now. Neither of these options involves Jesus having meant anything other than what he said, namely, that he considered John the greatest human being to ever have lived.

This does not mean that Jesus did not believe himself to be the stronger one of whom John spoke. Here the analogy between Elijah and Elisha may be particularly instructive. Elisha might be viewed as stronger than Elijah. He performed more miracles, and some might say greater miracles. Yet he did so as Elijah's disciple, and precisely as a result of having a double portion of Elijah's spirit. Elisha might or might not have said that he was stronger than his mentor Elijah. I doubt he would have said he was greater in a general sense.

Even if Jesus believed himself destined to occupy the status that Paul ascribes to him in Philippians 2:6–11 and 1 Corinthians 15:24–28, ruling over all creation subordinate to none but God the Father, that would not contradict or negate the force of Jesus's statement. That same passage in Philippians emphasizes Jesus's humility, and it is an axiom of Christian faith that Jesus was humble. Yet somehow when Christians find Jesus actually being humble and holding his mentor in higher esteem than himself, it seems unacceptable. If one denies that Jesus ever expressed such sentiments, one ends up emptying the claim about his humility of all meaning. John was so humble that he could envisage that one of his disciples would be so strong and so amazing that he would scarcely consider himself fit to untie his shoelaces as a slave might. Jesus, following his mentor's example, was able to esteem John above all other people that had ever lived, even while believing that it was his destiny to be that stronger disciple of whom John spoke. While some interpreters have tried to play John and Jesus off against one another, here perhaps more than anywhere else we see just how much they had in common.

Conclusion

This chapter more than any other makes clear why those in political and religious authority in John's time were concerned about him. Antipas feared his sway over crowds. The temple priests and those who taught torah saw a need to understand what he was claiming and on what basis. John offered a revolution in forgiveness, through a rite of immersion in flowing water. If John espoused and taught nonviolence, that would explain why others in his movement were not arrested and executed together with him at the same time. It does not, however, imply that John was not dangerous to their authority and their institutions in the way they correctly perceived. Not all prophets fostered regime change, much less extremely bloody and violent ones. All of them had the potential to, however, and that is why century after century, we find the powerful feeling threatened by those who have no institutional role and yet whose words have the power to move crowds to action. Today, those figures who were concerned about John's threat to their authority are remembered only because of their brief appearance in his story. This chapter has shown that the full extent of John's impact on his era has not been recognized by those who have written its history, whether ancient or modern. Even in relation to Jesus, the full extent of his influence has not always been recognized. John's relation to other figures, including not only the sign prophets but the ascetic Bannus with whom Josephus studied for a time, has been all but ignored.[14] As a result, his contribution to the events that led up to the Jewish war against Rome and the destruction of the temple, and his impact even if as a foil on those who found ways for Judaism to define itself without the temple after the events of AD 70, has not been appreciated. Given what we have seen here, that he ended up being executed by Herod Antipas is not at all surprising.

In the next chapter, we will look at the stories and traditions about how John met his end, and the impact that had on his movement (and the offshoots that emerged from it thereafter). Before proceeding, it is appropriate to address a question that many readers will have: Was Jesus the coming one of whom John spoke, or wasn't he? That is not a question that historical study can answer. A historian might, with the necessary evidence, be able to determine that John was or was not pleased with where Jesus took his movement and how things unfolded thereafter. Such evidence is lacking, not least because John died without seeing such things. Precisely because John was the leader of the movement and Jesus held him in such high esteem, there was no question of Jesus seeking to lead it prior to John's arrest. How much time passed between John's arrest and execution is difficult to determine, as is whether any information about his followers could have reached John while he was in custody. Moreover, the death of John influenced the direction of Jesus in profound ways, so that any vision Jesus might have had for the group before that may have been significantly revised.

There is, however, one thing that a historian can say in relation to this point. We do not know how famous John the Baptist would have been were it not for Jesus, but it is simply a historical fact that Jesus came to overshadow John so thoroughly that John is now thought of almost exclusively in connection with Jesus. No other follower of John does anything similar, much less anything "stronger." Mandaeans view Jesus as someone who departed radically from what his mentor John taught. Christians came to view John as predicting that Jesus would be precisely who he was. From the perspective of history, Jesus

---

14. Josephus's orders to his troops (*Life* 47) are strikingly reminiscent of the teaching of John the Baptist to soldiers in Luke 3. See further Christoph G. Müller, *Mehr als ein Prophet: Die Charakterzeichnung Johannes des Täufers im lukanischen Erzählwerk*, Herders Biblische Studien (Freiburg im Breisgau: Herder, 2001), 174–75.

was a follower of John and held him in high esteem. We can say with great confidence on that basis that Jesus *sought* to be faithful to John, to lead his movement where John would have wanted it to go. To the extent that he saw himself as the stronger one who was to come, he would have done so in a manner that he believed to be faithful to John's vision.

While some of John's group were disappointed after Jesus's execution, having expected the coming one to be victorious, it is only because things unfolded as they did that Jesus (and along with him John) is familiar in every corner of the world. If John's role as Christmaker was not what many readers of the Gospels have understood or assumed, and if Jesus's status as the coming one was not something John had a chance to offer his own opinion on, the two still hang together historically, with a strength that surpasses what any of their contemporaries achieved. John's vision, as Jesus and then his followers reinterpreted it, may not have brought in the kingdom of God in the form most who heard that phrase in their time would have expected. A historian cannot tell you whether that will eventually come to pass. But historically speaking, John has influenced the world, and the extent of his reach is due largely to the way Jesus, one who came after him as a disciple, surpassed him (John 1:30).

Many have sought to portray John and Jesus as though they were at odds with one another. Time and time again as I've investigated those possibilities, I have found at most superficial differences that didn't constitute disagreements. In each and every case, there was an underlying unity. If there was one point of genuine disagreement between John and Jesus, it was this: John said that one of his disciples would be someone so impressive that he himself would not even deserve to be his slave (Matt. 3:11; Luke 3:16; John 1:27). Jesus, on the other hand, said that no disciple can be greater than his master, although a good student can become like his teacher (Matt. 10:24–26 // Luke 6:40). Yet even here there is an undercurrent of similarity. Both John and his most famous student were humble. Even as Jesus sought to step into the shoes of that one whose shoe strap John said he wasn't fit to untie, he insisted that no student is greater than his teacher. The agreement in humility and esteeming others better than themselves as a point of agreement seems to me to outweigh the differences.

The Last Days

M artin Kähler famously described the Gospel of Mark as "a passion narrative with an extended introduction."[1] If we were to take all of the material about John the Baptist found in the Gospels and assemble it into a single narrative, the same could be said. We have a very brief summary of his message, a few details about clothing and diet, with this or that gospel adding some additional dialogue or ethical teaching. Then we have the famous story—found in Mark 6:14–29 and reproduced in Matthew 14:1–12—of Herod's birthday party, a dance, a foolish promise, and how these converged to bring about the death of John the Baptist. The story of John's death and the events leading up to it have taken on a life of their own in numerous famous paintings, Oscar Wilde's play, Richard Strauss's opera, and many other works of art.[2] The best-known elements of the story—the dance of Salome (a name not provided in Mark), Herod's promise, and John's head on a platter—are the ones about which a historian has the most reason to be skeptical.[3]

1. Martin Kähler, *The So-Called Historical Jesus and the Historic, Biblical Christ*, Seminar Editions (Philadelphia: Fortress, 1964), 80n11.

2. On the reception of the beheading of John, see, among others, Ulrich B. Müller, *Johannes der Täufer: Jüdischer Prophet und Wegbereiter Jesu* (Leipzig: Evangelische Verlagsanstalt, 2002), 210–19; Roger Aus, *Water into Wine and the Beheading of John the Baptist*, Brown Judaic Studies 150 (Atlanta: Scholars Press, 1988), 39.

3. See, on the other hand, William Chester Jordan, "Salome in the Middle Ages," *Jewish History* 26 (2012): 6–7, who pokes fun at the hypercritical stance of some modern historical scholars.

The biggest issues with the historicity are not, however, the ones that have immediately sprung to mind for some commentators. For instance, it is true that it is difficult to imagine Herod Antipas, client ruler of the Romans, offering half of his kingdom when he did not have the authority to do so. Nor, for that matter, was the domain over which Antipas ruled a kingdom. Contrary to the language Mark uses (6:14, 23), Antipas wasn't king, and thus his domain was not a kingdom but rather a tetrarchy, consisting of just two territories (Galilee and Perea, also known as Transjordan) that had been part of his father's larger kingdom. That objection is not as strong as it might initially seem, given the setting of the story at Antipas's birthday banquet. A wise and sober tetrarch, we might feel confident, would not promise anything up to half his kingdom to a dancing girl. There is no telling what an inebriated one might do. Despite Mark's claim (6:20), which we have reason to doubt, that Herod liked to listen to John, we can be reasonably certain that Herod did not emulate John's abstinence from fermented beverages. There might, of course, be other reasons to doubt that Antipas would make such a promise. For instance, the offer contains a striking echo of king Ahasuerus's offer of half his kingdom to Esther (Esther 5:3). This has led some to view that detail as an example of literary borrowing rather than historical information.[4] It is nevertheless possible to tell a story about actual events and use allusions to Scripture when doing so (as we see throughout the Gospels).

There are in fact much deeper and more substantial reasons to suspect that this famous story is a concoction by Mark. While the girl who dances has come to be casually referred to as Salome, that name does not appear in Mark's story. Different manuscripts of the Gospel of Mark give different impressions about whether the girl is an unnamed daughter of Herodias, or a daughter of Herod Antipas's named Herodias. The identification of the character in Mark's story

4. Nicole Duran, "Having Men for Dinner: Deadly Banquets and Biblical Women," *Biblical Theology Bulletin* 35 (2005): 122–23, https://doi.org/10.1177/01461079050350040101. The attempts of Aus, *Water into Wine*, to find parallels in Jewish expansions of the banquet of Ahasuerus in Esther, with no regard to their date, coupled with a latching on to even slender verbal parallels, results in an unpersuasive case overall. This is not to say that some details in the Markan narrative, such as a king promising half his kingdom (Esther 5:3), may not be drawn from Esther. However, given the late date of many of the retellings Aus mentions, it becomes possible that those stories were influenced by the story of John the Baptist's death, rather than vice versa.

with any specific individual mentioned in other sources faces many problems.[5] The daughters of both Herodias (from her first marriage) and Antipas seem, on the basis of the information Josephus provides, to be either too old or too young to fit the description in Mark in the relevant time period. Not that we can assume that Josephus consistently has correct information, of course. However, Josephus offers a string of details relating to Herod Antipas, his marriages, Roman governors, and the death of the emperor that hang together nicely. When we try to add the information from the Gospels into the equation, things become very puzzling indeed. Based on where Josephus tells the story of Antipas having John killed, and the usual dates for the crucifixion of Jesus, some have even suggested that John was executed after Jesus was. Others have tried to keep the sequence by suggesting that Jesus's crucifixion took place later than the preferred dates of AD 30 or 33.[6] Something is amiss, and it is hard to tell precisely what. This is not the place for a detour into chronology that considers all the relevant options, which would require discussion not only of the Gospels and Josephus but also Paul's letters, Acts, and other sources.

It is not just a few details but the whole history of the period, from the reign of Herod the Great to the spread of Christianity with Paul's involvement, that all need to hang together in relation to the story of John.[7] To do justice to

5. Ross S. Kraemer, "Implicating Herodias and Her Daughter in the Death of John the Baptizer: A (Christian) Theological Strategy?," *Journal of Biblical Literature* 125 (2006): 322–40, https://doi.org/10.2307/27638363, explores the key issues and finds all attempts to harmonize Josephus and Mark to face serious problems. Another problem to note is that according to Josephus, it is Salome who was married to Philip the tetrarch, the brother of Antipas, whereas Herodias's first husband was another brother whom Josephus simply called Herod (often designated Herod II to distinguish him from his father, Herod the Great). There is nothing in any source from that period outside of the New Testament to indicate that Herod II was known as Herod Philip, and while it is understandable how all of these brothers might bear the name Herod after their father, it is unlikely that two brothers would both be named Philip. On this, see further Nathan L. Shedd, *A Dangerous Parting: The Beheading of John the Baptist in Early Christian Memory* (Waco, TX: Baylor University Press, 2021), 11n33.

6. See Helen K. Bond, "Dating the Death of Jesus: Memory and the Religious Imagination," *New Testament Studies* 59 (2013): 461–75, https://doi.org/10.1017/S0028688513000131, for a discussion of the evidence and the range of possible dates.

7. One matter that it would be particularly helpful to be able to ascertain is the precise timing of the introduction of Roman shields into Jerusalem, a Jewish protest with Anti-

the question, we would ideally also need to discuss the editorial work of the gospel authors and the possibility that behind them stand still earlier sources that might have given a different impression. Even after a lengthy discussion, we might feel things are no clearer than they were at the outset. The truth is that, in the absence of modern set calendars, people regularly got the timing of events wrong when describing things that happened some years or even decades earlier. Add to this that some of the events mentioned, such as Passover in connection with Jesus's crucifixion, depended on observation of the moon (since Jewish festivals follow their traditional lunar calendar), and there is a lot of room for ambiguity. That is true even apart from challenges like the contradiction between John and the Synoptics about whether Jesus ate the Passover with his disciples and then was crucified, or was crucified on Passover (or perhaps the day before, right when the Passover lambs were being slaughtered). If you're feeling tired after part of a paragraph merely listed some of the issues, imagine how you'd feel if we actually tried to work through each of them and solve them.

Let's back up a bit. We did not, prior to this point, bring up the fact that Luke's reference to John having made his public appearance in the fifteenth year of the reign of Tiberius Caesar would most naturally indicate around AD 28–29, which many have felt to be too late to encompass Jesus's baptism and a period of public activity prior to his crucifixion. It may be that Luke's mention of Herod the Great in connection with the birth of John, and then the census of Quirinius taken after Herod died as the context for the birth of Jesus, indicates that some years passed between the birth of John and the birth of Jesus. That would stand at odds, however, with his assertion that John and Jesus were both in their mothers' wombs at the same time (Luke 1:41). The impression that John was significantly older might be at least approximately correct, with Luke's other statement being an attempt to make John seem more like Jesus's peer than his elder.

The fifteenth year of Tiberius also stands in tension with the reference to forty-six years of renovation work having passed at the time of Jesus's temple

---

pas and his siblings at the head, and the resulting imperial rebuke of Pontius Pilate. See Gideon Fuks, "Again on the Episode of the Gilded Roman Shields at Jerusalem," *Harvard Theological Review* 75 (1982): 503–7; Bruce Chilton, *The Herods: Murder, Politics, and the Art of Succession* (Minneapolis: Fortress, 2021), 161–62, https://doi.org/10.2307/j.ctv1khdnxr.

action (John 2:20). If construction began in or around 20 BC as is usually held, that brings us to several years before AD 29. Even if we posit (as some have) a reckoning of Tiberius's reign from when he did so alongside Caesar Augustus prior to his death, these details do not match up easily. As you can see, it is not as though the choice is between the New Testament and Josephus. There are problems within and between the New Testament documents as sources. This does not mean that they can be dismissed, but it does call into question the reliability of chronological information.

In light of what we have discussed here all too briefly, hopefully at least one thing is clear. We cannot simply accept the information Luke provides about the timing of events simply because he offers us a precise number and does so with confidence. Confirming evidence is required. When we lack it, or when other sources suggest a different timing, the best we can do is to offer possibilities, coupled with cautionary warnings about their uncertainty. Luke was capable of being wrong, just like every historian, ancient or modern, just as he also proves on many occasions his capacity to get things right. We should not make more of this than is appropriate, any more than we ought to minimize it. Even within our own lifetimes, we can sometimes feel certain that two things happened in the same year, until we are shown photographs and newspaper clippings that prove us wrong. Before there were either photographs or newspapers, there was much less opportunity to be corrected.

Whatever the precise date when his public work began, the overall impression we get is nonetheless likely correct: John was active for far longer than many have assumed. Christian readers of the Gospels have treated John as a brief flash in the pan before Jesus shows up, the opening act before Jesus performs his full set as the main attraction. In fact, it is most likely that John had multiple years of activity before Jesus joined his group, after which there were a few further years with Jesus himself part of John's movement, at which point John was arrested and, within a year or so after that, Jesus was arrested. Despite the great many difficulties in pinning down precise dates and correlating sources, and despite uncertainties and incongruities in our sources, there is a general flow of events in relation to one another that we must posit. Attempted solutions that fail to do this create far more problems than they solve. John appeared, Jesus joined him, and they worked together for a while. John was arrested and executed after criticizing Antipas; Jesus took on a leadership role in John's movement and was arrested and executed by the Romans.

Attempts have been made to avoid some of the tensions and contradictions by having John the Baptist outlive Jesus, for instance, or having the relationship between John and Jesus be a later fiction. Such solutions may satisfy some but fail to account adequately for how Christian literature could so quickly and uniformly converge on giving a different (and apparently wrong) impression, one that makes good overall sense in a way that alternatives simply do not.

Some at this point decide to do whatever it takes to harmonize the sources, creating an authoritative narrative that isn't what any individual source says. Others abandon the effort to pursue history and opt to treat each text as literature while setting aside questions about actual events. Neither of these alternatives should be considered appealing by anyone who considers it worthwhile to pursue knowledge and understanding about the past. Here we have sought to adopt what seems to be a better approach, seeking the gist of what was remembered as that which is most likely correct, while recognizing that individual details can and will be wrong in any source (some more than others, to be sure). Not only would cracking all these puzzles require a very different sort of book (one that few readers of biographies would enjoy plowing through); it would be unlikely to help us get a clearer sense of John's *story*.

That John met his end as a result of a decision by Herod Antipas to eliminate him is clear. Starting from that core piece of information, we can trace other threads and seek to bring into focus other major details. Inevitably some details will lose their sharpness as our lens focuses here or there. Magnification is a form of distortion, after all. We cannot hope to see a historical figure two thousand years ago any more clearly than a distant nebula. When we look at those stunning images from the Hubble and Webb Telescopes, it is easy to forget that often we are not seeing what the telescope captured but a colorized version, often representing things that are in the infrared range that the human eye could not perceive. Moreover, the image we see is itself an image of the past, not what we would see if we were in the vicinity of the object thousands of light years away, since the light takes that long to reach us. In much the same way, a biographer takes the black-and-white sketch from historical sources and seeks to add color. We cannot offer photographs or a memoir, but that doesn't mean the image that results from our efforts does not convey something true about the object of our investigation.

So let us turn now to what Josephus actually says. He tells the story of John's death in the context of Antipas's defeat by the Arabian king Aretas, father of Antipas's first wife whom he had decided to divorce in order to marry

Herodias. After adding that some people viewed Antipas's defeat as divine retribution for his execution of John, Josephus continues,

> Herod had put him to death, though he was a good man and had exhorted the Jews to lead righteous lives, to practise justice towards their fellows and piety towards God, and so doing to join in baptism. In his view this was a necessary preliminary if baptism was to be acceptable to God. They must not employ it to gain pardon for whatever sins they committed, but as a consecration of the body implying that the soul was already thoroughly cleansed by right behaviour. When others too joined the crowds about him, because they were aroused to the highest degree by his sermons, Herod became alarmed. Eloquence that had so great an effect on mankind might lead to some form of sedition, for it looked as if they would be guided by John in everything that they did. Herod decided therefore that it would be much better to strike first and be rid of him before his work led to an uprising, than to wait for an upheaval, get involved in a difficult situation and see his mistake. Though John, because of Herod's suspicions, was brought in chains to Machaerus, the stronghold that we have previously mentioned, and there put to death, yet the verdict of the Jews was that the destruction visited upon Herod's army was a vindication of John, since God saw fit to inflict such a blow on Herod. (*Jewish Antiquities* 18.116–119)[8]

The flashback to John's execution was natural in the context of Antipas's later defeat. The public associated the two because John had criticized Herod's divorce and remarriage, actions that ultimately led to the war with Aretas and Antipas's defeat. The fact that Antipas's decision dragged his people into a war may have been the main reason John objected so strongly to what Antipas had done, as we have already mentioned.

Some feel that Antipas's divorce must have led very quickly to outright warfare, but that is not necessarily the case. Others posit, in the interest of harmonizing Josephus and the Gospels, a period of escalating tensions between Antipas and Aretas before the full-scale military conflict in which the latter eventually defeated the former.[9] We do not need to resolve these matters to get

8. Trans. Louis H. Feldman in Josephus, *Jewish Antiquities 18–19*, Loeb Classical Library (Cambridge, MA: Harvard University Press, 1965), 81–85.

9. For a helpful brief discussion of the difficulties and their possible solutions, see Joel

the gist of what our various sources convey clearly. Crowds were paying close attention to John, John was critical of Herod Antipas and his marriage, and thus Antipas paid attention to John and decided to eliminate him. We can be reasonably certain that, if full-scale military conflict had not already broken out in John's time, some indication of its inevitability was already present during the time of John's activity. To be sure, an insightful person like John might not have required anything more than Antipas's divorce of Phasaelis to be sure there would be war between Antipas and Aretas. On the other hand, the urgent apocalyptic tone of John's warning that judgment was coming and repentance was needed might fit better in a time of actual warfare or of escalating tensions that are heading all too clearly in that direction. Either way, John likely lived long enough to see at least the beginning of the conflict. His declamations of Antipas for his action encouraged others to take a negative view of Antipas. It makes good historical sense that this, followed by Antipas's capture and execution of John, would lead people to view Antipas's defeat by Aretas as John's vindication, whether it happened soon after or several years later.

The Gospel of Mark seeks to shift the blame for John's death away from Antipas, and the political context and ramifications of Antipas's marriage are not mentioned (although they would undoubtedly have been familiar to readers). Mark's depiction of Antipas as taking a favorable view of John places his story in tension with what both the Gospel of Matthew and Josephus agree in saying, namely, that Antipas wanted John dead. Given the context and the combined information from our various sources, it is clear that Mark's account is less plausible than the others on this point. The story of Herod's execution of John is not the only place where Mark offers a narrative of this sort, one in which an authority figure, ultimately representing Roman rule, condemns someone to die, and yet the gospel author insists that their hands were tied and they really would have preferred not to execute the beloved leader of this religious movement. In the case of Herod Antipas and John, Mark shifts the blame to Herodias and her daughter.[10] In the case of Pontius Pilate and Jesus, Mark shifts the blame onto the Jewish authorities (Mark 15:1–15). In both stories, the presence of a larger group of witnesses, whether dinner guests or a crowd,

Marcus, *John the Baptist in History and Theology* (Columbia: University of South Carolina Press, 2018), 121–24.

10. Jennifer Lassley Knight, "Herodias, Salomé, and John the Baptist's Beheading," *International Social Science Review* 93 (2017): 1–15.

leads the authority figure in question to reluctantly give in to the demand that the person be condemned to die.[11] Historians have long judged it historically implausible that Pilate was eager to release a Jewish messianic figure who held sway with the crowds. The same applies to the notion that Antipas did not really want to execute John the Baptist.

As we have seen throughout this book, what became Christianity was a continuation or offshoot of the Baptist movement. The author of the Gospel of Mark is doing damage control, attempting to claim that despite the historically undeniable facts that John and Jesus were executed, it wasn't because the members of their movement were troublemakers. Their leaders were condemned and executed, but unjustly. The depiction of both events bears some relation to historical events, to be sure, but is reworked in the interest of apologetics and self-defense.[12] The point is not "this is what really happened" but "here is why, despite what everyone knows happened, the authorities should leave us alone." We must keep this in mind as we consider how John met his end and how that impacted those closest to him.

One reason for historical skepticism in the case of Jesus does not apply to John, however. Historians regularly point out that the followers of Jesus are unlikely to have had any contacts in Pilate's entourage who could inform them about any aspect of the proceedings that did not transpire publicly in the view of all. In the case of John and Herod's birthday celebration, on the other hand, we must note that one of the sponsors of Jesus's activity was Joanna, the wife of Antipas's property manager Chuza (Luke 8:3). Now, Chuza is a Nabataean name, and Antipas had divorced his Nabataean first wife to marry Herodias. It may be that Chuza and Joanna were no longer part of the entourage of Antipas by this point. Nevertheless, they would have maintained contacts in Herod's household.

All of this leads to the conclusion that it is not impossible that what happened to John in those fateful days was witnessed and transmitted to Jesus and

11. Shedd, *Dangerous Parting*, 92–93.

12. On the connection between the deaths of John and Jesus in Mark, see Shedd, *Dangerous Parting*, 21, 56, 92–99. Shedd writes of the keying of John's beheading to Jesus's crucifixion, but surely the reverse makes more sense both historically and within the chronological framework of the narrative. The more familiar event of John's execution is used to interpret that of Jesus. Because Jesus's crucifixion is the more familiar event today, it is perhaps understandable why it is instinctive to begin there, but we must resist that instinct in contextualizing Mark's narrative in its own time.

those associated with him. This doesn't mean that what Mark wrote is in fact what happened, just that he could have been well informed, and if he was, then he could have told us what happened if he wished to. There is a lot of potential and possibility there, as you can see, but also a great deal of uncertainty. Whether Mark knew things and, if so, how much of that he included in his story must be judged on the basis of that story, how plausible it is historically, and how well it fits with other reliable historical information that we have.

Ironically, the one thing most people would say they know about John with some confidence—the dramatic story of his death—turns out to be unlikely to have happened in the form in which everyone has heard it. This is all the more ironic when we consider that so much about John that can be deduced with some confidence has not been explored or become widely known. This is a perennial challenge in ancient history. Past events are often more clearly discernible through deduction from snippets of passing references than from that one vivid and memorable story that, although told early and repeated often, turns out to bear little resemblance to what actually happened. Even in those instances, however, memories and traditions that are more accurate may emerge and become visible against the tide. Josephus tells us that Antipas wanted to kill John, and Matthew agrees (Matt. 14:5), despite the fact that he was using Mark as a source. Luke goes further still, initially narrating only about Herod arresting John (Luke 3:19–20), mentioning his beheading only later (Luke 9:9), and in neither instance is the blame shifted to Herodias or anyone else.[13]

Mark's story of John's death and the events leading up to it comes rather out of the blue, interrupting the flow of the narrative as an unanticipated flashback. Once Mark mentioned Herod's puzzlement at what he heard about Jesus, and his wondering whether perhaps Jesus was John returned from the dead, Mark would have likely remembered that he had not told that story. He may have felt he needed to, but on the other hand, the death of John was likely common knowledge and thus could be merely alluded to. Mark chose to tell the story because it could serve a useful purpose. He could offer a narrative in which he cast the event in a less unfavorable light and deflected blame away from those

13. On the identity of the girl who dances according to Mark's story, see Wim J. C. Weren, "Herodias and Salome in Mark's Story about the Beheading of John the Baptist," *HTS Theological Studies* 75 (2019): art. 5573, pp. 1–3, https://doi.org/10.4102/hts.v75i4.5573.

in political power whose verdict cast an ominous shadow over the ongoing movement. That Mark reworks tradition and invents new material does not mean that what he wrote becomes of no value for the investigation of the historical John the Baptist. In general, even apologetically motivated stories can be useful to the historian. They are simply useful in different ways and for different reasons, compared to other kinds of material. For one thing, in the process of telling this story, Mark clues us in to just how similar Jesus seemed to John in the eyes of their contemporaries.

MACHAERUS, MASADA, AND TIBERIAS

Josephus tells us that Herod Antipas had John executed at Machaerus, a desert fortress (*Jewish Antiquities* 18.5.2). That any place of potential imprisonment is mentioned leaves open the possibility that the Gospel of Mark is correct about that detail, that Antipas arrested John but then kept him alive for at least a little while after his arrest. The idea that he did so out of admiration, however, is extremely unlikely. Indeed, it would have been expected that Antipas would have killed John immediately. Possible reasons for Antipas keeping John alive for a while that are historically plausible include wanting to find out more about his movement and his followers, in order to better ascertain the extent of the threat and deal with it effectively. Prior to his execution, we can be fairly certain that John would have been tortured in an effort to learn more about his movement. That John would have been allowed visitors in prison is extremely unlikely. It is only Matthew who gives us the impression that this might have happened, by placing the Q story about John sending messengers to Jesus in the context of John's imprisonment (Matt. 11:2). The Q source did not mention John's imprisonment, as far as we can tell. If there is any historical basis to the story, it may simply reflect a time when John and Jesus were active in different places.

Today relatively few people take the time to visit Machaerus in Jordan, while its twin in Israel, Masada, is an extremely popular destination for tourists. The reason for the difference is not only the availability of a cable car at Masada to make the trip to the top much easier. The provision of that means of ascent is a consequence of the greater interest in visiting the site. In John's time, Masada was in Judea, and after Archelaus the son of Herod the Great was deposed, it became a Roman stronghold. Then, in the context of the Jewish war against Rome in the second half of the first century AD, it was taken over by Judeans, and not only soldiers but families took refuge there. When the Roman forces besieged it as the last holdout at the end of the war, the majority of inhabitants killed their families and then themselves, according to the famous story, with only a handful of women and children remaining in hiding, found there when the Romans at last managed to capture it. Today it serves not only as a tourist attraction but as a symbol of Jewish national pride. Today many Israeli soldiers take their oath at Masada, and even those who do not mention it, swearing that "Masada will not fall again." Machaerus, on the other hand, today lies in the neighboring country of Jordan. It had a shared history in the eras of the Hasmoneans and then the time of Herod the Great, but after his death, his kingdom was split among his children so that these two similar fortresses would have different histories thereafter. Machaerus was in Antipas's territory, while Masada was not. The fortresses of Herod the Great, like the pieces of his kingdom, were divided up and separated from one another. The symbolism of that was even more poignant once Antipas's brother Archelaus was deposed from ruling over Judea and Samaria.

Antipas didn't build Machaerus, but he did undertake building projects elsewhere, including a new capital city for his territory located in Galilee. During my Holy Land trip, I visited the new capital city that Herod Antipas built along the lake, which he named Tiberias after the emperor. It eventually gave its name to the lake so that it came to be known as Lake Tiberias, although other names also remained popular. If the story about Herod celebrating his birthday by holding "a banquet for his courtiers and officers and for the leaders of Galilee" (Mark 6:21) has any basis in history, the banquet would without question have taken place in Tiberias. There is no conceivable reason why he would have asked leaders in Galilee to gather not at his capital in Galilee but in the distant and remote fortress near the Dead Sea.[14] Combining the information we have leaves us with several options. One is that Josephus was incorrect about where John was imprisoned. It would indeed have been rather strange for Antipas to have John brought there, given that that was where his first wife (whom he divorced to marry Herodias) went prior to fleeing home to Arabia, Machaerus being located right at the border with that neighboring territory

14. Aus, *Water into Wine*, 41–42, 48.

with which Antipas now found himself in conflict. Perhaps the symbolism of killing John, the critic of his divorce of his Arabian wife, there near the border of Arabia seemed symbolically important to Antipas.

It may also be that the story in Mark is mostly or entirely fabricated. Those who wish to preserve both also have an option. In Mark's story, we are not told that the platter with the head of John the Baptist was brought in while the birthday meal was still taking place. There is no reason why the birthday party could not have taken place in Tiberias and, upon the order of the tetrarch, men were dispatched to carry out the execution of John, who was imprisoned in Machaerus. Again, if there is any truth at all to the story, we should not imagine Antipas being forced against his will to execute John but deciding to do so, perhaps as a result of conversations and council taken with the leading men of Galilee. More likely, he did not require any persuading. That Herodias might have wanted John's head on a platter is not the implausible part of Mark's story. That part rings true.[15] What is implausible is the notion that it would have required some exceptional circumstances, plotting, and dancing to bring it about. Beheading was often the mode of execution in cases of insurrection and competing claimants to a throne. The Romans had famously beheaded the last member of the Hasmonean dynasty to lay claim to the title of king, when the Romans instead supported the competing claim of Herod the Great, Antipas's father. If anyone had been thinking that John might be able to take Antipas's place, this would remind them what had happened to others who had tried to stand in the way of the Herodians.

Matthew 14:12–13 claims that John's disciples took charge of his body and gave it the required burial. Torah requires that the dead be buried before sundown. It is entirely plausible, indeed most probable, that Antipas would have ensured that this was done.[16] Whether he would have allowed the disciples to

15. The fact that John the Baptist had styled himself as another Elijah might have led Mark (or someone before him) to depict Antipas's wife as particularly eager to see the prophet John put to death, just as in the case of Jezebel with the prophet Elijah. That Mark fabricated the story does not mean that she was not eager for this critic to be silenced, just as her husband would have been.

16. On execution and burial in a Roman context, see Mark D. Smith, "The Final Days of Jesus and the Realities of Roman Capital Punishment: What Happened to All Those Bodies?," *Bible and Interpretation*, February 2018, https://bibleinterp.arizona.edu/articles /2018/02/smi428014#sdfootnote5sym.

collect John's body and give it whatever sort of burial they thought he deserved is less plausible. Indeed, since Machaerus was rather remote, for Herod to hand John's body over to his disciples for burial, he would probably have had to send word to them prior to John's beheading. Perhaps he did just that, getting a message to them that he planned to release John to them, with the intention of having them witness John's execution and take care of his body, while also carrying the news as a warning to John's wider movement. The message was twofold: I have cut off the head not only of John but of your movement, and I know where to find you.

It may be, on the other hand, that (as later tradition would claim) a sympathizer or secret disciple of John was present in Herod's household and able to arrange for John's disciples to provide burial for John's body or head, or both. This may not have been done openly, or right away. Whoever it was might have been able to send word to John's other disciples about where Herod had had the body buried. At some later point, they came to remove John's remains and bury them elsewhere in the manner they thought he deserved (see Matt. 14:12). On the other hand, if the corpse was delivered to them without the head, in order to serve as a message and warning, that might have provided the seed for speculation and stories about the circumstances that led to John's beheading, just as the later church would tell many stories about what John's head got up to in the years and centuries thereafter. While there are several different locations that each claim to have John's head, the body of John is said to have been buried in the city of Samaria (modern Sebastiya), on a site where today there is a mosque. It is an intriguing tradition, given the evidence of John's impact in Samaria.[17]

It was natural, in light of what we have said above, for Antipas to respond to Jesus's appearance soon after as leader of the movement by wondering whether John might somehow have been raised from the dead. The beheading of John was supposed to be the beheading of the movement. The ongoing life of the movement with rumors of a living head was a message to Herod: you have not stopped John's movement, nor can you. Some have suggested that beheading was thought to be a means of preventing as definitively as possible resurrection or revivification.[18] This seems extremely unlikely, however, since resurrection

17. Jerome Murphy-O'Connor, "Sites Associated with John the Baptist," *Revue biblique* 112 (2005): 265–66.

18. Shedd, *Dangerous Parting*, 15–16, 22, 73–77, 88.

itself required a miracle of reconstitution of which only God was capable, and it seems hard to believe that those who believed that even death would not prevent God from rewarding his faithful added a disclaimer, "except in cases of beheading." That, of course, referred to the resurrection of the age to come, the new creation in which all things might be possible. Reviving a beheaded individual in this life, on the other hand, was another matter, and that kind of magic or miracle might indeed have been considered impossible. In an era before modern technology, it was disturbingly frequent for people to be thought dead when they in fact were not. Beheading left no doubt. If Herod contemplated that the things he heard about Jesus might indicate John had risen from the dead, even if he was not inclined to believe that to be the case, it tells us something crucial about John. His reputation was such, as far as the divine power thought to be at work in and through him was concerned, that even the seemingly impossible could not be altogether ruled out in his case.[19]

In the Wilderness Again

Other than Mark's "immediately" in 1:12 (which he uses so often that we could be forgiven for suspecting that the author thought it simply meant "then"), there isn't a particularly strong basis for concluding that Jesus's time facing temptations in the wilderness depicted in the Synoptic Gospels followed right after his baptism. Indeed, the entire scene as it is elaborated in Matthew and Luke (and thus presumably in Q) is more symbolic than literal, depicting Jesus as obeying precisely where the book of Deuteronomy says the people of Israel had disobeyed in the wilderness. John had castigated the nation with the wilderness as his backdrop, for continuing the tradition of grumbling and disobeying that had begun in their wilderness wanderings after the exodus. He called them to return to the wilderness and make a choice different from

19. Kraemer, "Implicating Herodias," 341–44, makes the case that Antipas asked a question rather than made a statement: "Is John whom I beheaded raised from the dead?" Whether Matt. 18:8 indicates that Jesus himself believed that disfigurement in this world remained in the world to come is difficult to say, as the statement may be hyperbolic and counterfactual: if losing a foot or an eye meant you lost it forever and would not have it restored even in the resurrection, that would still be preferable to the alternative of punishment in the age to come.

that of their ancestors. To depict Jesus as entering the wilderness, facing the temptations the nation had faced, and refusing to give in to them was to depict Jesus as John's ideal follower, and as such his natural successor as leader to the movement. That is how early Christian authors told the story, setting it immediately after Jesus's baptism and prior to his public activity independent of John. In fact, a lengthy period of involvement by Jesus in John's movement may have been what followed, as the Gospel of John indicates.

The arrest and execution of John would have moved Jesus into a wilderness experience and may have sent him to return to an area of wilderness literally as well as metaphorically. John's death forced him to wrestle with his own path and where it might be leading him. The temptation story depicts Jesus following John in baptism and in the wilderness and then embracing and living out the values that John had taught, so that Jesus emerges as John's ideal follower and natural successor. Mark's Gospel goes on to say that, after John was arrested, Jesus came back into Galilee and (in light of what it says in the Gospel of John) regrouped his followers. How much of this John was aware of we cannot tell, but as we have already mentioned, it is extremely unlikely that Herod Antipas allowed John to have visitors in Machaerus. The impression that John sent a message to Jesus from prison to ask whether he is the coming one is a result of the Gospel of Matthew combining elements from Mark and Q.

Perhaps we should nonetheless take a lesson from the Gospel of Mark's preferred phrasing and emphasize the fast pace with which things likely unfolded. After several years of activity, Jesus's temple action had drawn the attention not only of the authorities in Jerusalem but of Herod Antipas. Although Jerusalem was not in Antipas's territory, John was regularly in Antipas's domain and had crowds eagerly listening to him there. If John could persuade some of his followers to cause a disruption in the heart of Jerusalem, he could do likewise at Tiberias. Antipas would have been a fool to wait and see what happens. He had John apprehended. Then he may have waited to see whether that caused the movement to disperse, holding John hostage, as it were, both to try to elicit information about other leading figures in the movement and to see whether the arrest of John and prospect of his execution was enough to put the movement in its place. Jesus's regrouping of John's followers resulted in Antipas hearing that the movement continued, and so Antipas had John executed. The continuing ripples that Jesus made, and the attention he started to get as leader of the movement, prompted Antipas to wonder whether even decapitation was not sufficient to get rid of John. He seemed to have returned from the dead. This confirms for us very clearly that the activities of Jesus in this period closely resembled those of John. Were that not the case, Antipas's reaction would have been different.

Matthew 14:12–13 says that, when he was informed of John's death, Jesus withdrew to a remote place, literally a wilderness place. Given John's symbolic and literal connection with the wilderness, no other action would have seemed appropriate. The death of John would have had an enormous impact on Jesus and presumably equally on others among John's followers. The overall flow of the Gospels conveys the impression that it was John's martyrdom above all else that led Jesus to consider that his path might lead him to a similar fate. Yet the death of John was not a theological problem for his followers in precisely the way that Jesus's was. John's message is the reason why. As far as we know, nothing that John had said about himself constituted a promise that he would not meet with a violent end. To be sure, some may have seen in his styling himself as a new Elijah a hint that he, too, would be taken up to heaven without dying, in a fiery chariot or whirlwind (2 Kings 2:11–12), but we have no indication that John said anything along those lines. Jesus's supporters, on the other hand, viewed him as the one to whom John had pointed, who was expected to enact judgment and be demonstrably victorious over the wicked. After John's death, Jesus came to see his mission as more similar to John's than most of John's followers thought it was supposed to be.

Intriguingly, a Jewish work known as the Assumption of Moses envisaged a Jewish father encouraging his sons to be willing to be martyrs for the specific reason that if they did, it would provoke a response from God, who would then bring in his kingdom. If Jesus considered that he and John (whether as a new Elijah and Elisha, the priestly and royal messiahs, or simply God's faithful prophets) might, by being willing to humbly and obediently sacrifice their lives without either fleeing or resorting to violence, bring about the arrival of God's kingdom, he may not have been the first to do so. In the view of most scholars, the Assumption of Moses was edited and finalized with updates to make Moses predict not just earlier persecutions of the people of God but the Herodian rulers. Whether those who found this text relevant to that specific time were members of John's movement, and whether Jesus himself might have read or heard about the text, we cannot hope to know. Nor do we need to. Ideas circulate even among those who have not read a particular work. Even in our era of widespread literacy and availability of books, many more people speak of paradigm shifts than have read Thomas Kuhn, or about deconstruction than have read Jacques Derrida. The first century was different from ours in many ways, but this was not one of them. The fact that we find something in a text from a given era does not mean that it was widely known, but when we see evidence of an idea circulating so that it appears in more than one text, we are justified to posit influence or at least a shared milieu of ideas.

Whether that author and Jesus came up with the idea independently, or one influenced the other, doesn't change what we see happening. From this moment on, we find Jesus increasingly speaking and acting as one who expected to suffer at the hands of authorities. Although historians are understandably skeptical of claims that Jesus foresaw his death ahead of time and interpreted it in a theological manner, he would not have needed to be a prophet who received divine revelations, much less anything more than that, in order to see that if he took up the mantle of leading John's movement, he would almost certainly meet the same fate as John had. This did not require supernatural knowledge of the sort that a historian cannot appeal to. It required only observation, intuition, and foresight of a sort that it is perfectly reasonable to believe Jesus had. Once he was forced to ponder the prospect of his own death while simultaneously trying to make sense of that of his mentor, it would have been natural, perhaps inevitable, for Jesus to turn to the Scriptures and to the teaching of John to make sense of these things. Had Jesus not done so, historically speaking, there is little chance that he would be remembered today as having been so very different from the sign prophets and other such figures. Had he not been different, in other words, he would probably not be much remembered, never mind revered. What set Jesus apart, historically, is that he did not march forth promising victory only to meet with defeat. Others did that, were killed, and became a passing mention in history books. If Jesus had not provided enough hints that his path to filling the role of the stronger one would be the path John himself had followed, the way of suffering, then the cognitive dissonance caused by his death would have been too overwhelming for anyone to make sense of it.

By proclaiming that a stronger one would emerge from among his followers, John became the Christmaker. Through his death, John began to shift into the role of forerunner of the suffering Messiah. That was not because he had seen himself that way or spoke of a coming one who would be like that but because John's death changed Jesus's understanding of how he was to pursue the destiny that he believed lay before him. John's death, as Jesus came to understand it and to understand his own in light of it, became the foundation upon which the Christian church would later build its theology, developed to make sense of the seeming oxymoron of a crucified yet victorious king.

SEEING JOHN VINDICATED

Jesus was not the only one in John's movement to wrestle with John's death and what it meant for their hopes and expectations. The hints we find of followers of John in later times who considered him the messiah, or who told stories that envisaged the possibility that he would rule Israel, all suggest that death did not mean the end for others in John's movement either. While some looked to Jesus as the one who was to come, others apparently came to believe that John himself would be brought back by God to himself serve as the stronger one. It is impossible to know whether this happened right away or was a result of followers of John seeing what the followers of Jesus had done after his death and applying the same approach to John.

Mandaean sources, interestingly enough, do not describe John dying violently. In their account of John's death, a celestial messenger comes to John and simply removes the garment of flesh and blood from him. John is troubled, and when asked why, it is not for himself but for his children, who are full of zeal but will not have him to teach them. In Mandaean tradition, John marries and has children. It is not impossible that there is some historical basis for that. Once we get away from the idea of John as an ascetic hermit, many of the strongest potential objections disappear. As in the case of Jesus, the earliest evidence simply does not tell us one way or the other about marital status. If there was a Baptist movement led by members of John's family, just as Jesus's brothers played a major role in the developing church in Judea and Galilee, both of those failed to survive in the long term, and their histories are now largely obscured in the mists of time. Be that as it may, the Mandaean version of the death of John represents a gnostic angle on the appropriate view of death in general. Their version of the story may have been developed to serve two purposes simultaneously, helping at the same time to mitigate the trauma of John's death and to address the issue of human mortality more generally.[20]

20. On this, see further Charles Häberl, "The Mandaean Death of John," in *Alpha: Stud-*

The Christian tradition preserves stories about Herod the Great martyring John's father, Zechariah, in the temple. On one level, this is likely based on a misunderstanding of Jesus's words about all the martyrs from Abel to Zechariah (Luke 11:51 // Matt. 23:35). Jesus had referred in that saying to the death of a priest and prophet in the temple who was mentioned in the Jewish Scriptures (2 Chron. 24:17–25).[21] When he did so, he probably had the murder of John the Baptist on his mind. Just as God had finally had enough when the nation killed yet another prophet, and swiftly brought judgment that included the destruction of Jerusalem and its temple, Jesus believed the same would come upon this generation. Jesus had spoken of the temple's demise before, but he returned to the theme and emphasized it again toward the end, as the story of Judah's past resonated with his own understanding of John and himself in the present. Killing John was the last straw, which would cause God to recall all the others who had gone before him and been unjustly killed.

The story that Christians told about Zechariah probably evolved out of a story that was originally about John. The shift to his father may have been an intentional reinterpretation or just the natural process whereby events associated with a less central and well-known place come to be connected with somewhere more famous. Christians recalled Jesus's words about the blood of martyrs from Abel to Zechariah crying out for justice, told as commentary on the murder of John. They interpreted Aretas's destruction of Machaerus where John's blood had been spilt as God's retribution against Antipas. John's blood had cried out for justice, and God had delivered. Later, after the destruction of Jerusalem and its temple in AD 70, the story was recast as about those places, and the saying of Jesus about Zechariah assisted the process of turning the story about John into one about his father, who had been a priest that served in the temple, the one the Romans later destroyed. While we saw John and his father, Zechariah, at odds with one another at the beginning of this story of John's life, in the imagination of later Christians, Zechariah became something of a precursor for John, dying a martyr's death precisely to protect him from Herod the Great, who wanted to kill him. Like father, like son, they say, but in this case, the process is better described as like son, like father.

---

ies in Early Christianity, ed. Alvin P. Cohen, Glenn S. Holland, and E. Bruce Brooks (Amherst, MA: Warring States Project, 2017), 1:35–36, https://doi.org/10.2307/j.ctvcwp0mv.

21. Edmon L. Gallagher, "The Blood from Abel to Zechariah in the History of Interpretation," *New Testament Studies* 60 (2014): 121–38, https://doi.org/10.1017/S0028688513000246.

It was the conviction of Jesus's followers that he had been vindicated beyond death through bodily resurrection as the start of the life of the age to come that resulted in him not becoming just one of a string of figures listed by Josephus as having made a stir in this era. Few told stories about John's vindication in an afterlife, but some did. Some saw John vindicated in what befell Herod Antipas. For the most part, if we can speak of John's vindication, it is as a result of the way his impact lived on through the others who were grasped by his message, took it up, and made it their own. If John is rightly remembered as saying that one who came after him would show such strength that he himself would seem an unworthy slave by comparison, then I can only imagine that John would be happy with how things unfolded.

John did not start an organization. One might even offer the critical evaluation that, based on the evidence we have, his goals were ill defined. He did not seek fame or to draw attention to himself, other than for the purpose of sharing his teaching and calling people to repent and be baptized. He was so influential in his time and throughout time because he had a vision that was at once so simple and yet so profound. He longed to see forgiveness flow freely. He longed to see "justice roll down like water and righteousness like an everflowing stream" (Amos 5:24). While not everyone shared that vision then or now, many do even today—including some who may not have a full sense of the extent to which they and the tradition to which they belong are indebted to John the Baptist. Not that he was completely innovative. No one ever is. Creating new and powerful music that will stand the test of time rarely if ever involves inventing new instruments and making sounds that have never before been heard. It is even more challenging to take notes that we all have listened to countless times before and arrange them in a new way that somehow has the power to move our hearts, to touch our spirits, and to stick in our minds. Familiar notes, yet a new song that stands out as something special, such as has never been before and may never be again. Something that, if it loses its distinctiveness, will be because so many who follow after will imitate it and make us grow weary of it. That is who John was and what he did. He was by no means the first prophet of repentance, righteousness, and forgiveness, nor would he be the last. If John taught, and himself embodied, the kind of genuine humility that truly esteemed others as greater than himself, so that he has been overshadowed and his distinctive voice lost in the mix, then he deserves to be dragged back into the limelight, even if it must be done against his will.

CONCLUSION

Even if we have had reason to question the traditional story about John's death, the key point remains, namely, that he was apprehended and killed on orders from Herod Antipas. This book as a whole, and in particular this chapter, has filled in the details of how that conflict came about and why it ended with John's death. Only Mark insists that Herod did not wish to kill John and was forced to. It is probably not a coincidence that Mark is also the first to present the execution of Jesus by the Roman official Pontius Pilate in the same way. Both Herod Antipas the tetrarch and Pilate acquiesce to the demands of others according to this our earliest Gospel. This was likely a strategic move with an apologetic aim, seeking to present the Christian movement as not a political threat, its leaders having been put to death for reasons other than that they were stirring up trouble for authorities. Thus it was that the most famous story about John came to be told, overshadowing the story of his life in much the same way that the cross of Jesus would come to take center stage in the message Christians proclaimed about him.

Today, Antipas's capital city, Tiberias, has a population of less than fifty thousand. It is no longer the capital of anything. There is very little to see there that connects with the distant past, and none of it is from the time of Antipas. There is an underdeveloped archaeological park where the original city once stood, which gets few visitors and very little attention. Within the modern city, there are other ruins and a few historic buildings you can see here and there, which might give you the illusion of catching glimpses of the era of John and Antipas. All of those, however, date from much later times than the one we have been exploring, and even those are not well maintained or the focus of much attention from tourists. If you go to Tiberias hoping to see glimpses of architecture that convey even a vague sense of what the city was like in John's era, the completely new capital that Antipas had built, you will be disappointed. There is nothing grandiose and impressive to see, and no pilgrims flock to such ruins as there are. As I walked around the city looking at these places, I could not help but wonder whether Herod Antipas could ever have imagined that his greatness would be forgotten despite all his construction projects, while the troublemaker he executed would be far more famous than he. He certainly never imagined in his wildest dreams that people would travel from all over the world to visit sites with only a hint of a legendary connection to John, while the places Antipas himself built and renovated lay neglected ruins. Had anyone suggested that his name might be remembered only as part of the story of John the Baptist, would he have become angry, or merely laughed because the notion was so utterly ridiculous?

Archaeologist Jerome Murphy-O'Connor wrote about Antipas's capital city, Tiberias, "Herod Antipas's choice of a virgin site betrays his desire to emulate his famous father. He wanted to create a showplace that would be entirely his own."[22] Just as Zechariah is known because of his son John, and John is remembered by all but a few due to his association with Jesus, Herod the Great and his son Herod Antipas are likewise remembered largely due to their associations with John and Jesus.

Before concluding this chapter on John's final days, and turning in the final chapter to tracing the ripples of John's impact that have since his time reached every corner of the globe, it is fitting to reflect on who is remembered and why, how one's role in history may become all but forgotten except for a bit part in someone else's story. The Herodians played an important role in the history of their people. They were not hated by most people in their time. Their building projects and navigation of political challenges had an impact on their subjects that was not always positive, but neither was it disastrous. We find it hard to think of them as anything more than flat villains in a familiar drama. It is impossible to think highly of an ancient figure when all you know about them are stories about innocent lives being cut short on their orders. A political leader in our time whose enemies are disappeared may be justly despised and condemned, but they may still be visible as more of a well-rounded figure than any ancient figure can hope to be.

One thing that Antipas and John share in common is that each is remembered largely for his role in the story of Jesus. A close examination shows that Antipas's interest in Jesus was a result of his prior interest in John and Jesus's association with him. Hopefully the exploration of the life of John the Baptist we have offered here has already made clear how differently we may understand the life of Jesus if we pay John the attention that he deserves. Unless we seek as full a portrait of not just John but Antipas and many other individuals who seem like extras in the story of Jesus, we not only will fail to understand

---

22. Jerome Murphy-O'Connor, *The Holy Land: An Oxford Archaeological Guide from Earliest Times to 1700*, Oxford Archaeological Guides (Oxford: Oxford University Press, 2008), 515. See also Murphy-O'Connor, "Sites Associated with John the Baptist."

them but will fail to understand Jesus as well. As this book has shown, Jesus is himself one example of the important positive impact of John in human history. He is not the only one, and the concluding chapter will trace other lines of influence. Doing so is relevant in the context of a biography of this sort, since it helps us get a better sense of John's historical significance.

For ripples to continue spreading even into our time, the impact of John's life two thousand years ago must have been enormous. Rather like those who marvel at the beautiful clouds of gas that result from a supernova, we may forget that once there was a star that burned brightly, whose existence is responsible for the expanding nebula we now see. John "was a burning and shining lamp, and you were willing to rejoice for a while in his light" (John 5:35). In the next chapter, we will see just how much that light remains visible and continues to shine, even if indirectly, in fires lit from his original flame.

No One Is Greater Than John

A s we reach the final chapter in this biography, we look beyond the death of John and his immediate impact to survey the wider ripples that his life caused, trajectories of influence that will carry us to the ends of the earth and from John's time all the way to the present, with no indication that his influence will cease any time soon. We thus take as our starting point, and as the title for the chapter, Jesus's emphatic statement that John was the greatest human being who ever lived (Matt. 11:11 // Luke 7:28). As we trace the ripples of John's impact beyond his immediate contemporaries, we find that Jesus's high praise was no exaggeration. There is no continent and no country where John's impact has not been felt at least indirectly. In view of the profound impact John had on Jesus, in theory it might suffice to point to the global impact Christianity has had and leave the matter at that. That is indeed part of John's impact, but it is not the whole story. If only because some would rightly say that the impact of Christianity reflects the influence of Jesus and of Paul at least as much as of John, it is important to show that Christianity is not the only means by which John's impact has been felt, or the only route by which his influence remains present in our world to this day.

We had many opportunities throughout this book to ask what Jesus learned from John, so that we could use those things to fill in our portrait of the Baptist. We saw early on that the Lord's Prayer and its focus on God as Father reflect the way John taught his disciples to pray. Much of the ethical teaching of Jesus, and his view of the temple and forgiveness, also owe much to John. John's teaching about baptism as an alternative to sacrifice played an important role in shaping Christian soteriology—that is to say, the doctrine of atonement and how salvation is understood to be accomplished. Christians retained baptism but turned it into a onetime act of conversion to identify with Jesus in his death and resurrection. The idea that animal sacrifice could be foregone and done away with because Jesus had offered his own obedient life to God as the ultimate sacrifice built on the foundation that John had laid, even as it went very far beyond it.

Jesus was an innovator, even in relation to John, whom he esteemed so highly and to whom he owed so much. Early in the book, we mentioned the complaints people lodged against John, that he came "neither eating nor drinking," while Jesus came "eating and drinking" and they complained about him, too. One possible point of contrast to which this might allude has to do with fasting. The gospel tradition mentions people noting that John the Baptist's disciples fasted just as the Pharisees fasted, while Jesus's disciples did not. This seems like an obvious and indeed a stark contrast between John and Jesus, and it has led New Testament scholar John Dominic Crossan to emphasize the difference between "a fasting John and a feasting Jesus."[1] This way of putting things, however, ignores what Jesus actually taught his disciples about fasting. It wasn't to cease doing so and thus break with Jewish tradition. It was to *hide* the fact that they were doing so, so that only God would know, and thus they would be rewarded by God rather than by the esteem shown to them by others for their meritorious actions. This means that when people asked why Jesus's disciples did not fast, the reality was that they *were* fasting but hiding the fact. Jesus's deflection is in keeping with the fact that the point is for others not to know this is what is happening, so that only God knows and thus God alone will reward the action. This was clearly an innovation on the part of Jesus, to emphasize hiding the good that one did from the view of others. It was an innovation that built on John's core teachings rather than departed from them. It was a difference, not a disagreement. Time and time again, when we think we see a stark contrast between John and Jesus, it is much more likely that there is a deeper continuity than we realize.

There are also places where the views of those who remained allied to John but rejected Jesus have had an impact, through the need that various New Tes-

---

1. John Dominic Crossan, *Jesus: A Revolutionary Biography* (New York: HarperCollins, 2009), 48.

tament authors felt to respond to their views. There are clear examples of this in the Gospel of John. In the Gospels of Mark and Luke, the good news began with John the Baptist. In the prologue of the Gospel of John (John 1:1–18), the author still brings John the Baptist on the scene as the first human character to appear. Yet the author seeks to elevate Jesus in relation to John by going all the way back to "in the beginning," presenting the Word as becoming flesh in the human life of Jesus. The author thereby presents Jesus's exaltation to the right hand of God as a return of the now incarnate Word to where it was before. John the Baptist, in contrast, is emphatically not the light (1:8). The number of times the author feels it is necessary to repeat the point indicates that there were others who thought otherwise.

Other details in the Gospel of John are also readily intelligible as polemic against followers of John who thought they had no need of Jesus. If John embodied the spirit of Elijah, and Elijah had journeyed to heaven, then surely John could reveal heavenly things. The author of the gospel insists that no one has actually gone up into heaven except the Son of Man, who came down from heaven (John 3:13). It is hard to imagine that the author really wanted to deny all other claims of heavenly ascent, although it is not explicit in the Scriptures where individuals like Enoch and Elijah went. Perhaps the author of that gospel really did mean that no one else ascended at all, and would have disputed Paul's claim about a journey to the third heaven (2 Cor. 12:2). The worldview of that era envisaged multiple spheres around the earth, which lay at the center. At the very least, the author of the Gospel of John believed that Jesus was the only one who had ascended to the highest heaven, not for a mere visit but to remain there at God's right hand (or, to use that author's metaphor, in God's bosom). This was not merely possible but appropriate in his case because he did not embody the spirit of Elijah or some other human being but united in his person the preexistent Messiah described in the Parables of Enoch, and the very Word of God that was God's instrument in creation according to Genesis.

In other gospels, related concerns come up, albeit in different ways, so that it is clear that while all the early Christian authors were concerned to say something about the relationship between John and Jesus, they did so in different ways. The accounts of John baptizing Jesus also illustrate this. In Mark, our earliest gospel, we are simply told that it happened. Matthew has John insist that he needs Jesus to baptize him rather than vice versa. Luke moves the mention of John's imprisonment immediately prior to Jesus's baptism, thus distancing

Jesus's baptism from John's authority as baptizer. The Gospel of John doesn't explicitly narrate John baptizing Jesus but merely says that John baptized in order that Jesus might be revealed.

The infancy stories in Matthew and Luke (as well as those in other Christian infancy stories outside the New Testament, in particular the Infancy Gospel of James) also owe something to the back-and-forth between members of the Baptist movement who allied with Jesus and those who did not. We get a sense of this in the manner that Luke draws on storytelling about the Baptist that had already begun in the circles of John's followers, and adds alongside John similar stories about Jesus. In the Gospel of Matthew, it is less obvious that this has occurred. When, however, we bring the Infancy Gospel of James into the picture, we see that this must have been the case. After telling stories about Mary's parents, Mary and Joseph, and the birth of Jesus, we are suddenly told that Herod was searching for John, which leads Elizabeth to flee with him into the wilderness. Herod voices the reason for seeking the son of Zechariah, which is concern that John is destined to rule Israel. This is clearly a fragment of an infancy story created by followers of John the Baptist, since Christians would not invent a story in which John was sought because of the possibility that he was destined to replace Herod. We need not take time here to try to figure out which came first and which followed later. The important point is that followers of the Baptist told stories focused on John similar to the ones Christians told about Jesus. Who started it isn't important, although given that John's movement precedes any independent movement focused on Jesus, it is more likely that John's followers crafted stories about John first. Either way, the competition between those who focused exclusively on John and those who owed allegiance first and foremost to Jesus led both groups to develop stories in which they not only depicted one or the other as great but sought to outdo the portraits of the other.

We thus get a narrative and theological arms race that drove the development not just of Christian storytelling but of Christology, that is, the understanding of the person of Jesus in Christianity. It is hard to know at times whether a particular difference in the literary depictions of Jesus and John, whether in Christian or other sources, is about the historical figures being different or their later followers. For the most part, the strong sense of competition does not appear to go back to the time of John and Jesus. Indeed, Jesus's words of praise concerning John prevented most Christians from denigrating

John. Their only option was to elevate Jesus higher still so that John's greatness paled in comparison.

Some branches of the early Christian movement stood much closer in their connection to John the Baptist than others. One group called the Elchasaites practiced repeated baptisms and emphasized the power of baptism to effect not only forgiveness but healing. The most famous individual who grew up in that movement was Mani, after whom the religion of Manichaeism is named.[2] Mani rejected the baptismal practice with which he was raised, even though he himself apparently had a powerful religious experience in connection with the ritual. He became aware of his celestial counterpart but understood this as a call to become the latest in a long line of apostles. The religion he developed was a universal one, able to draw on other religions far and wide while claiming to offer something more than any of them did. He spread his religion quite effectively, so that it reached China, where its impact can still be seen to this day.[3] Although he became famous as a Christian church leader, Augustine was a Manichaean prior to his conversion.[4] Both the faith he previously espoused and that to which he shifted were influenced by John the Baptist. Whether that influence was prized or repudiated doesn't matter. The point is the extent to which major moments in the history of religion, and of human society and thought more generally, have been shaped in one way or another by the interaction of movements that took at least something of their impetus from John. While we cannot explore here the influence of Augustine's thought, particularly on topics such as original sin, the fact that almost every reader will have heard that phrase says enough. In the examples considered thus far, we see that John's influence in various forms reached China, North Africa, Meso-

2. Werner Sundermann, "What Has Come Down to Us from Manicheism?," in *Light against Darkness: Dualism in Ancient Mediterranean Religion and the Contemporary World*, ed. Armin Lange et al., Journal of Ancient Judaism Supplements 2 (Göttingen: Vandenhoeck & Ruprecht, 2010), 226–48, https://doi.org/10.13109/9783666550164.226.

3. It was the official religion among the Uyghur people of central Asia during one period of their history in late antiquity.

4. For more on this, see Jason D. BeDuhn, "'Not to Depart from Christ': Augustine between 'Manichaean' and 'Catholic' Christianity," *HTS Theological Studies* 69 (2013): art. 1355, pp. 1–8, http://dx.doi.org/10.4102/hts.v69i1.1355. Since Manichaeism emerged from a form of Christianity and included Jesus along with other figures within its system, some categorize it as a form of Christianity.

potamia, and, of course, every place in which this book is being read. Yet even so, we haven't exhausted the lines of impact that need to be drawn to convey the full extent of John's legacy.

Our ancient sources all agree that John made waves in his time, within the context of his own Jewish people and religious tradition. The population was drawn to him. Yet ultimately in the mainstream of Judaism, other movements than his played the biggest role in determining the direction in which they flowed. Even so, there is no question that John played a role, both directly and indirectly. Christianity and developing rabbinic Judaism were involved in a process of mutual self-definition in this era, and as a result, it can be difficult to spot points at which John's influence may be seen independently. Once again, we should not merely note the impact of Christianity as part of the broader influence of John and move on. Rabbinic sources composed and compiled over the course of centuries, in the Holy Land and in Babylonia, mention "morning immersers" or "daily bathers" who sound like they had a practice like that which John promoted, as evidenced by groups like the Mandaeans and Elchasaites. Ancient Christian authors also mention "daily baptizers" as one of the Jewish sects, and the Pseudo-Clementine literature says John was associated with that movement. To this day, there are Jews in the Hasidic tradition who immerse themselves before prayers in keeping with that ancient tradition associated with John.

We mentioned earlier that some have suggested the Jewish practice of proselyte baptism might have influenced John. In fact, the reverse is far more likely. That influence may have been indirect, by way of Christianity and its baptism, but since there would be no Christian baptism were it not for John, that in no way diminishes the point. What originally was the highly symbolic first ritual purity immersion by a gentile who was joining the people of Israel increasingly became a symbolic act in its own right with connotations of rebirth. John's emphasis on God providing alternatives to animal sacrifice also provided ideas that other strands of Judaism were able to use when figuring out their own way to navigate life in the wake of the destruction of the temple in Jerusalem.

The Samaritans, on the other hand, had learned to cope with the destruction of their own temple on Mount Gerizim some centuries earlier, worshiping on the sacred place even in the absence of a sanctuary. John undoubtedly learned from his activities among the Samaritans as well as having an impact among them. We saw that two individuals from Samaria among his disciples,

Dositheus and Simon, are connected with the origin of Gnosticism. Dositheus himself, like John, does not seem to have been a gnostic but only someone whose activities led to its emergence. We have evidence of a Dustan (i.e., Dosithean) sect among the Samaritans. One of their characteristic practices makes clear that this is indeed the same Dositheus who was affiliated with John the Baptist. They had the custom of praying while standing in water and venerated its cleansing power.[5]

Even though tradition places John's tomb in Samaria, he is little known there today among the Samaritans. When I visited Samaria, I was taken around their important sites by a wonderful tour guide named Abood Cohen. As in Judaism, so too among the Samaritans, that surname indicates being from a priestly family. Unlike in Judaism, the Samaritans still celebrate the Passover by sacrificing a large number of lambs. This is done on Mount Gerizim, just as would have been true in John's time. Yet the traditional site of John's tomb in Sebastiya (i.e., ancient Sebaste, the city formerly named Samaria) was a place he had never visited, as far as we know. Today the site is a mosque, and that is not surprising, since John is a prophet in Islam as well. The name Sebaste represents the Greek term whose Latin equivalent is Augustus. Caesar Augustus gave Herod control of the city, and in return, Herod renamed it in the emperor's honor. The city's older name Samaria was eventually given to the entire kingdom after the Israelite king Omri moved his capital there. It was during the reign of Omri's son Ahab that Elijah appeared to challenge him. The city thus has multiple layers of connection with John, and even if there isn't any strong evidence that John's disciples reclaimed his body and buried it there, it is nevertheless a fitting location for a tomb in his honor. John the new Elijah is revered today in the capital city of the king against whom the original Elijah stood.

John's connections with Islam go back to its very beginnings. On the one hand, the earliest stories we have about Muhammad indicate that he knew and lived close to Christians. By the time the Qur'an reaches the form in which we now know it, the Mandaeans were also known to the nascent Muslim community. They are mentioned alongside Jews as people of the book under the name Sabians, meaning "baptizers." Between them and perhaps also the

---

5. For this information from Abu'l Fath, see Stanley Jerome Isser, *The Dositheans: A Samaritan Sect in Late Antiquity* (Leiden: Brill, 1976), 79, https://brill.com/view/title/3261.

Manichaeans, Islam had prototypes to draw on for alternatives to the dominant Abrahamic traditions in the Arabian peninsula, Judaism and Christianity. These alternative religious traditions said Jews and Christians were both wrong while also being partly right. They envisaged a long line of prophets that God had sent, including some outside the boundaries of Judaism and Christianity. John seems to have given a spark to a proliferation of prophetic-type figures that continued beyond the instances we mentioned close to his lifetime, such as Jesus and the sign prophets. That idea, embodied in John, others inspired by him, and still others inspired by his successors and imitators, has continued to influence the development of new religious traditions ever since.

Islam's Scriptures and subsequent storytelling also incorporated tales of John himself as well as his father, Zechariah. I remember well when I visited a tomb that was regarded by Byzantine Christians as being that of Zechariah, the father of John the Baptist. Located in the Kidron Valley that lies between the old city of Jerusalem and the Mount of Olives, it came to be called in Jewish tradition the Tomb of Absalom instead. Historically speaking, neither figure is likely buried there. As we have seen throughout this book, the lack of a genuine historical connection with John the Baptist does not appear to have any detrimental effect on pilgrimage. As I was coming from visiting the location, I passed a couple of Muslim men who asked whether I could help them find the location of the tomb of the prophet Zechariah. I pointed the way, happy to have this illustration of the significance of John and his family for Muslims.

One of the things this book included that is typically neglected is an exploration of John's connections with the origins of Gnosticism. While the Mandaeans are especially interesting because of the way they hold John in high regard, John's influence is not only on that particular Mesopotamian branch of Gnosticism but on the phenomenon as a whole. Baptism is mentioned in many of the Coptic gnostic texts found at Nag Hammadi in Egypt. John the Baptist himself is mentioned in some of them. The tractate called the Three Forms of First Thought (Trimorphic Protennoia) promises those who undergo the baptismal ritual, "the Baptists will baptize you and you will become gloriously glorious" (45.12–20).[6] Scholars debate whether baptism in Gnosticism was a

6. Trans. John D. Turner, "Trimorphic Protennoia," *Gnostic Society Library*, http://gnosis.org/naghamm/trimorph-JDT.html. Quoted and discussed in Harold W. Attridge, "On Becoming an Angel: Rival Baptismal Theologies at Colossae," in *Religious*

literal rite involving water or something spiritual. Most likely it was both, with baptism in water the means to the deeper experience. The Secret Book of James has Jesus refer to the beheading of John as the cutting off of the head of prophecy itself. The Secret Book of John (named after Jesus's disciple rather than the Baptist) not only features sealing through baptism, but the very origin of creation begins when the supreme God sees the divine reflection in waters of light, which mirrors the kind of experience we suggested that John might have had, and encouraged others to have, in and through baptism. The Paraphrase of Shem speaks of a demonic baptism that appears to distract from the true baptism, in language reminiscent of how Mandaean sources view Christian baptism, as a distortion of John's original rite. Mandaean baptism offers the possibility of glimpsing the ancient gnostic ritual as a living practice. How much it may have evolved over the centuries is hard to say, but it still includes elements that are mentioned or hinted at in ancient sources, including sealing with oil as well as water, the placement of a sprig of myrtle as a symbolic crown, and the consumption of water and bread.

While the Mandaeans are not widely known today—certainly not as widely known as they deserve to be, given how fascinating and distinctive their tradition is—that has not always been the case. The Theosophical movement was sparked at least in part by the translation of the Mandaean sacred text known as the Great Treasure into Latin. For those unfamiliar with Theosophy, it is a major precursor to what became known in the twentieth century as the New Age movement, an eclectic approach to spirituality that draws on Eastern religions as well as those that historically predominated in Europe and the Americas. Matthew Norberg translated the Great Treasure (Ginza Rabba) from Mandaic (a dialect of Aramaic) into Latin, which was published in 1816. Helen Blavatsky, the driving force behind Theosophy, refers to that Mandaean sacred text in her books. The Mandaeans use the term "Nasorean" to denote someone adept in the esoteric knowledge of that tradition. Blavatsky took that (as have a number of others) to indicate that Jesus, rather than being a Nazarene, was a Nasorean, an adept of this mystical tradition. The similarities between many details in the systems of Mandaean and Jewish mysticism encouraged Blavatsky as well

Propaganda and Missionary Competition in the New Testament World, ed. Lukas Bormann, Kelly Del Tredici, and Angela Standhartinger (Leiden: Brill, 1994), 488, https://doi.org/10 .1163/9789004267084_024.

as others since to seek a spiritual truth that transcended any one tradition and could be discovered by taking what one found agreeable from many. Historically, the similarities are a clue that Mandaean and Jewish history at one point coincided. While for some, the separation came about early on, it is likely that for others, there was a long history as an esoteric movement within a Jewish community, before the differences caused a rift and a departure. The close affinities between gnostic ideas and Jewish mysticism show that there is a shared tradition. It would be going too far to posit a central role for John himself in creating and developing some of the key facets of those traditions. But his activity clearly did, at the very least, provide them with a spark and catalyst that contributed to their very existence as well as their impact.

Encounter with Mandaeans may also have influenced European art. In many paintings, John holds a cross-shaped staff with a scroll draped like a banner upon it. Although I have tried to trace the origin of this element in visual depictions of John, I have not been able to determine the earliest example. This standard feature in paintings of John bears a striking resemblance to the staff with a crossbeam that Mandaean priests plant in the river when performing baptisms. In Mandaeism, it is the banner that is the symbol, representing the lightworld and the connection that rivers offer with the world above. The crossbeam is merely there to support it. For Christians, the resemblance to the cross of Jesus is striking indeed. I suspect that some artist or other centuries ago had an opportunity to see a Mandaean baptism and drew the image from there. That the similarity is coincidental seems less likely. Christians clearly interacted with Mandaeans throughout history in the places where they found themselves close to one another. One example is the mention of a "baptism of Saint John" in a twelfth-century baptismal rite from Mesopotamia, a region where the Mandaeans have historically been found in significant numbers. This baptism of Saint John was something that was practiced by some Muslims, thought to offer them some kind of protection from evil yet not constituting conversion.[7] It seems unlikely that the notion of a baptism of Saint John, offer-

---

7. David G. K. Taylor, "The Syriac Baptism of St. John: A Christian Ritual of Protection for Muslim Children," in *The Late Antique World of Early Islam: Muslims among Christians and Jews in the East Mediterranean*, ed. Robert G. Hoyland (Berlin: Gerlach, 2021), 437–60, https://doi.org/10.2307/j.ctv1b9f5mn.21; Jack Tannous, *The Making of the Medieval Middle East* (Princeton: Princeton University Press, 2018), 235–36, https://doi.org/10.23943/princeton/9780691179094.003.0013.

ing spiritual benefits but not conversion to Christianity, could have developed in Mesopotamia where Mandaeans have historically lived, without their baptismal practice being at the very least a source of inspiration.

Mandaean texts are also worth mentioning as part of a rather unusual period in New Testament scholarship. During the early part of the twentieth century, some New Testament scholars responded to the publication of German translations of key Mandaean texts by positing these as the background against which to explain the New Testament. Scholars had been puzzled by the emphases in early Christianity, found in some texts more than others, on things that did not derive from and did not have parallels in rabbinic Judaism, their main source of knowledge of Judaism close to the time of Jesus. Given the prevailing anti-Semitism in Germany where this idea was spearheaded, it is probably no coincidence that many gravitated toward alternative sources for Christianity's key emphases. Since the Mandaeans were found in Iran, an Indo-European rather than Semitic background could be posited for Christianity's distinctive features. Or so they thought. As it turned out, rather ironically, the source of the core Mandaean ideas, their deepest ancestral heritage, was in ancient Israel, although obviously with additions courtesy of John the Baptist, interactions with developing mainstream Judaism, and other sources. Rather than eliminating a connection with Judaism by turning their attention to Mandaeans, they reinforced it. Not only John the Baptist and Jesus but the Mandaeans and Gnosticism turn out to have deep roots in the traditions of Israel—some of which became predominant, others of which persisted on the margins and in the shadows until John's activity brought them out into public view.

In another potentially ironic twist to the story, it was the discovery of the Dead Sea Scrolls that provided a means to explain the elements that seemed to come from elsewhere than Jewish orthodoxy. Indeed, that discovery made clearer than it had been that in the first century there was no Jewish orthodoxy but a range of ways of being Jewish and practicing Judaism, with points of commonality as well as differences among them. I said it was ironic that the discoveries at Qumran had this effect because, of course, the field of New Testament study shifted from associating John with Mandaeism to associating him with Qumran. Either way, John was clearly pivotal. As it happens, John's connection with Mandaeism as an influence upon it may be more direct than any influence of the Essenes on him. Either way, we are dealing with John's impact.

We have seen John's impact spread into the Arabian Peninsula, Mesopotamia, Persia, central Asia, and China in an eastward direction, while it simultaneously spread westward throughout the Roman Empire, including North Africa. It definitely also reached India, as evidenced by the Marthoma Church (i.e., the Church of Saint Thomas) there. Regardless of whether that church genuinely goes back to Jesus's apostle Thomas, the church in India appeared early in Christian history. At several times down the ages, Europeans have traveled there, planning to bring them the gospel, only to discover to their surprise that there were already Christians. Yet once again, it seems that there may be other influences from John besides those mediated through Christianity in this part of the world. When I started this research project, having been struck by the immersion practices I had seen when visiting Varanasi as well as in documentaries about India, I suspected that it might just be possible that an ancient tradition had traveled along the Silk Road from India to Israel and made a splash there, if you'll forgive the pun. This wasn't at all implausible, even if it might be difficult to prove. After all, the Hebrew word for peacock is believed to come from Tamil. There had been trade between India and the Mediterranean since long before John's time. The stories about the apostle Thomas traveling to India to proclaim the Christian message might or might not be true, but they were not beyond what was imaginable.[8] Yet as I investigated further, it turned out that these immersion practices did not go back to the Vedic era and the deepest roots of Hinduism.

While once again there were no clear answers to when these practices began in the Indian subcontinent as part of the worship of the traditional deities, at least some scholars I asked suggested they might be medieval in origin. I thus began to contemplate what had previously been unthinkable. Might this Hindu practice, too, reflect the influence of John the Baptist? With Elchasaites established in Mesopotamia and Mandaeans both there and in Persia well before the Middle Ages, one or more baptismal practices stemming from John the Baptist was available close by to be seen and borrowed. Neither this nor anything else set forth in this chapter, or indeed this book, should be taken to mean that there was influence from John upon others and not the reverse. Christians in India did not only influence that part of the world but reflect the influence of

8. On this, see James F. McGrath, "History and Fiction in the Acts of Thomas: The State of the Question," *Journal for the Study of the Pseudepigrapha* 17 (2008): 297–311, https://doi .org/10.1177/0951820708091899.

those around them.[9] That was no less true for Christianity as it spread into Europe. Influence is always dialogical, involving a back-and-forth.

In addition to John's direct impact on each of these traditions through his life, John's impact is also traceable through their interactions with one another. We have already seen some examples of this, but more can be added to the list. Much more. In addition to Christian baptism influencing Jewish proselyte baptism, we might mention Gnosticism influencing Marcionism, which in turn sparked the concerted effort to define the New Testament canon. Reaction against Gnosticism led to the development of the doctrine of creation out of nothing, which in turn framed the context in which Christians defined orthodoxy in terms of the Trinity. Other examples could be provided. Whether embraced or resisted, the ripples from John's impact intersected to further shape the course of religious history. When all of that is tallied, can there really be any denying that John was, if not the most influential figure in the history of religion, at least someone to be ranked in the top ten? Suggesting that such influencers be ranked is, of course, contrary to the spirit of what John said and did. Yet how else can we convey the extent to which he has been underappreciated? What analogies are there, apart from thinking of others getting number-one hits with cover versions of his songs?

There is no way to trace the full extent of John's impact. Just as so many details of him as a historical figure are lost to us due to the inevitable partial record keeping and the passage of time, so too the scope of his effect on human history is often inadequately documented or obscured by the fact that no one factor of influence ever stands on its own. Just as John's historical significance has often been obscured by those he inspired to come after him, the waves caused by the splash he made have, when combined with other factors or channeled down particular paths, managed to crest higher and higher, blocking our visibility as we seek to peer into the past and see where it all started.

Like the door that leads into the courtyard of the Church of Saint John the Baptist in Jerusalem, often what we are looking for has been so unobtrusive that we have walked right past it. That church in the souq (market)

---

9. See the helpful treatment in C. D. Sebastian, "Interaction between Classical Indian Ethics and Christian Ethics," in *History of Science, Philosophy, and Culture in Indian Civilization*, vol. 12, part 2, *A Historical-Developmental Study of Classical Indian Philosophy of Morals*, ed. Rajendra Prasad (New Delhi: Concept, 2009), 480–87.

in the Christian Quarter is literally as well as metaphorically overshadowed by the much bigger and more popular nearby Church of the Holy Sepulcher, which marks the place where Jesus is believed to have been crucified, buried, and raised from the dead. If you actually realize the Church of Saint John the Baptist is there and deserves your attention, you may well find the door to be locked. That church commemorating John seems a fitting place to conclude the final chapter of the book—hidden from view, overshadowed by the memory and the memorialization of Jesus, missed by those hurrying to see someone and something else. Yet John is there nonetheless, just like that church, with hidden depth that is worth exploring, if only we take the time, can figure out where to look, and can gain access. This book has sought to take care of that last part, bringing what has long been hidden and neglected into plain view. If you have read this far, I am certain that you have caught a glimpse of John, perhaps for the first time, or at least for the first time with this degree of clarity. I kept going back to that door in Jerusalem while I stayed in the city, hoping that one day I would be able to enter and glimpse behind it. I eventually did. I hope that my similar perseverance seeking the historical John the Baptist, and your perseverance reading this book to the end, has proved equally rewarding.

Epilogue

B iography, in one form or another, has been around since before the time of John the Baptist, although no one among his contemporaries wrote a biography of John per se. The Gospels offer snippets of biography, and the Mandaean Book of John's central section at least purports to do likewise. Yet already by that stage, and perhaps even earlier, they were starting to veer into another genre. By the time later Christian authors decided to elaborate further on John's story, we tend to refer to what they produced as hagiography to make clear that it bears no resemblance to the biographical aims of either ancient historians or modern ones. Hagiography literally means the telling of lives of saints, but the word is used in our time for any idealized portrait of someone. Ideological commitment can distort one's depiction and even motivate one to freely invent—and just as freely forget what is inconvenient. Ancient historians were aware of the danger. Yet even the best ancient biographies fail to provide the kinds of information that modern readers are most interested in. What was their education like growing up, and what was their relationship with their parents? What influences and experiences inspired them or traumatized them, shaping their psyche and motivating them to pursue the path that led to their becoming the kinds of figures people write and read biographies about? The difference between ancient biography and modern means that a modern biographer, writing about an ancient subject, either will disappoint their readers or will provide what readers want by deducing answers from source material that does not provide them directly or explicitly.

Modern books on John the Baptist have thus fallen into one of two categories. Some have been academic books engaged in an effort to recover aspects of the life of John, or to understand the early sources about him as literature and as theology. Others have been historical fiction, modern hagiography, that felt free in the absence of information to weave fanciful narratives. In the academic volume that I wrote simultaneously with this one, *John of History, Baptist of Faith*, I sought to offer a book in the aforementioned academic genre. I make the case there that we have neglected important sources of information and have missed the implications of details in the few sources that we have consistently turned to when seeking to study John. The aim in doing so was to provide a solid foundation that would make it possible to do something different in the volume you have just read, something that had not been done before at least in this form. *Christmaker* seeks to utilize the imagination but not in the manner of hagiography. Instead, the aim has been to use it in a very disciplined fashion to connect the dots between secure data points, between things we can say about John with a high degree of certainty, and to fill in the implicit context of that information. In doing so, a portrait begins to take shape. Then all that is left to do is narrate it.

As I stated in the introduction, most have considered it impossible to write a biography of John the Baptist. The chapters of this book may have persuaded you that they were right, or convinced you that they were wrong. Either way, it is worth considering that people do attempt, without similar criticism, to write a life of Jesus, or of Paul, or of countless other ancient figures. The existence of more ample early narrative sources does not necessarily mean those other cases are fundamentally different from that of John. Often we have more detailed ancient sources not because more information was preserved, and was preserved more accurately, but because ancient authors were interested and created narratives out of snippets of information in much the same manner as I have in this book. To be sure, there is always a benefit to having sources closer to the events transmit information across time to us. The efforts of past biographers, however, inevitably distort as well as transmit. Sometimes they are a lens that brings things into clearer focus, which is itself a form of distortion, even if a helpful one. At other times they have the opposite effect. If having multiple biographical sources for Jesus makes the task of the biographer and the historian easier in some respects, it also simultaneously makes it more difficult, as each author's interpretive lens becomes another potential hurdle to understanding even as it also provides the only means to glimpsing their subject and ours. Scarcity and abundance both have benefits and challenges.

It is my sincere hope that my efforts here to bring together neglected ev-idence and well-informed imagination will have served to produce a clearer and more accurate image of John. If not, I hope that at the very least I have provided an attempt that will lead others to correct my errors and do a better job than I did. The effort has persuaded me at its end even more than at the outset of a conviction that I have come to hold. It is not as though our choice is between history and imagination. Our only choice is between historically informed imagination and imagination unconstrained by historical evidence. People have imagined John the Baptist ever since his own time and have never ceased doing so down the ages. Some of those images familiar from paintings and movies are too little based in evidence and have distorted our perception of him. John was less recluse and wild man than an articulate intellectual of profound moral and spiritual vision. I hope that my book helps you to imagine that John, a John more like he really was than the typical portraits.

Whether John the Baptist is someone who stands within your own tra-dition or outside it, and whether you have read this book as an expression of historical interest, religious piety, or both, I hope that I have helped you to appreciate the significance of John. Yes, from our vantage point, we can see him as Christmaker, especially in relation to Jesus, but also as one whose own prophetic life and vision inspired would-be successors and imitators galore for centuries to come. If imitation is the sincerest form of flattery, the highest form of praise, then perhaps no one in history has been appreciated as much as John, if we include not only those who emulated him directly but also those who imitated those who themselves patterned their lives on John, his predictions, or both. I hope, however, that in the process of bringing John into focus as the Christmaker of the book's title, I have also enabled you to actually look at John closely and understand him, not just as a figure preliminary to someone else but as a fascinating and important individual in his own right.

Having tallied up just a sampling of the ripples of his impact in history, I hope that you will agree that John is more than the Christmaker. He is one of the most influential (or as they say today, impactful) people in the history of religion. He is not the focus of religious devotion per se in any of the traditions that are indebted to him, except in the sense that he is counted among the saints of Christianity and the martyrs and prophets of Islam, and people from these traditions make visits as pilgrims to sites associated with him. I don't have the impression that John would want that devotion. Nor do I think he would care much about historical appreciation. If I ask myself what John himself would want readers of a biography about him to take away with them, it is undoubtedly things along these lines:

- to be inspired and dedicated not to merely repeat the bad habits of our ancestors;
- to seek a life-changing encounter with the divine;
- to practice justice in ways that genuinely cost us, because we value the lives of others and see them as entitled as we are;
- to not treat forgiveness as though it provides an excuse for failing to do any or all of the above.

If this book leads you to do any of those things, then as the author of this biography, I can feel content knowing that I have indeed made John visible through the veil of centuries, so that the message he was willing to proclaim at the cost of his life resonates on and continues to be heard, even in our time.

Bibliography

Adler, Yonatan. *The Origins of Judaism: An Archaeological-Historical Reappraisal.* New Haven: Yale University Press, 2022.

Allison, Dale C. *Constructing Jesus: Memory, Imagination, and History.* Grand Rapids: Baker, 2010.

Attridge, Harold W. "On Becoming an Angel: Rival Baptismal Theologies at Colossae." In *Religious Propaganda and Missionary Competition in the New Testament World,* edited by Lukas Bormann, Kelly Del Tredici, and Angela Standhartinger, 481–98. Leiden: Brill, 1994. https://doi.org/10.1163/9789004267084_024.

Aus, Roger. *Water into Wine and the Beheading of John the Baptist.* Brown Judaic Studies 150. Atlanta: Scholars Press, 1988.

Backhaus, Knut. "Echoes from the Wilderness: The Historical John the Baptist." In *The Study of Jesus,* edited by Tom Holmén and Stanley E. Porter, 1747–85. Vol. 2 of *Handbook for the Study of the Historical Jesus.* Leiden: Brill, 2011.

Barnett, P. W. "The Jewish Sign Prophets—A.D. 40–70: Their Intentions and Origin." *New Testament Studies* 27 (1981): 679–97. https://doi.org/10.1017/S0028688500007165.

BeDuhn, Jason D. "'Not to Depart from Christ': Augustine between 'Manichaean' and 'Catholic' Christianity." *HTS Theological Studies* 69 (2013): art. 1355. http://dx.doi.org/10.4102/hts.v69i1.1355.

Bond, Helen K. "Dating the Death of Jesus: Memory and the Religious Imagination." *New Testament Studies* 59 (2013): 461–75. https://doi.org/10.1017/S0028688513000131.

Bovon, François. *Luke 1: A Commentary on the Gospel of Luke 1:1–9:50*. Translated by Christine M. Thomas. Minneapolis: Fortress, 2002. https://doi.org/10.2307/j.ctvb6v878.

Brattston, David. "The Forgiveness of Post-baptismal Sin in Ancient Christianity." *Churchman* 105 (1991): 332–49.

Buckley, Jorunn J. *The Mandaeans: Ancient Texts and Modern People*. New York: Oxford University Press, 2002.

Cameron, Alan. *The Last Pagans of Rome*. New York: Oxford University Press, 2010.

Cargill, Robert R. *Melchizedek, King of Sodom: How Scribes Invented the Biblical Priest-King*. New York: Oxford University Press, 2019. https://doi.org/10.1093/oso/9780190946968.001.0001.

Chilton, Bruce. *The Herods: Murder, Politics, and the Art of Succession*. Minneapolis: Fortress, 2021. https://doi.org/10.2307/j.ctv1khdnxr.

Crossan, John Dominic. *Jesus: A Revolutionary Biography*. New York: HarperCollins, 2009.

Drower, E. S. *The Mandaeans of Iraq and Iran: Their Cults, Customs, Magic Legends, and Folklore*. Piscataway, NJ: Gorgias, 2019. https://doi.org/10.31826/9781463208073.

Dunn, James D. G. "Jesus and Purity: An Ongoing Debate." *New Testament Studies* 48 (2002): 449–67. https://doi.org/10.1017/S0028688502000279.

Duran, Nicole. "Having Men for Dinner: Deadly Banquets and Biblical Women." *Biblical Theology Bulletin* 35 (2005): 117–24. https://doi.org/10.1177/01461079050350040101.

Edsall, Benjamin A. *The Reception of Paul and Early Christian Initiation: History and Hermeneutics*. Cambridge: Cambridge University Press, 2019.

Edwards, James R. *The Gospel according to Luke*. Pillar New Testament Commentary. Grand Rapids: Eerdmans, 2015.

Fuks, Gideon. "Again on the Episode of the Gilded Roman Shields at Jerusalem." *Harvard Theological Review* 75 (1982): 503–7.

Gallagher, Edmon L. "The Blood from Abel to Zechariah in the History of Interpretation." *New Testament Studies* 60 (2014): 121–38. https://doi.org/10.1017/S0028688513000246.

Gibson, Jeffrey. *The Disciples' Prayer: The Prayer Jesus Taught in Its Historical Setting*. Minneapolis: Fortress, 2015.

Gibson, Shimon. "On John the Baptist at the Jordan River: Geohistorical and Archaeological Considerations." In *Fountains of Wisdom: In Conversation with James H. Charlesworth*, edited by Gerbern S. Oegema, Henry W. Morisada Rietz, and Loren T. Stuckenbruck, 217–40. London: T&T Clark, 2022. http://www.bloomsburycollections.com/book/fountains-of-wisdom-in -conversation-with-james-h-charlesworth/ch15-on-john-the-baptist-at-the -jordan-river-geohistorical-and-archaeological-considerations/.

Häberl, Charles. "The Mandaean Death of John." In *Alpha: Studies in Early Christianity*, vol. 1, edited by Alvin P. Cohen, Glenn S. Holland, and E. Bruce Brooks, 35–36. Amherst, MA: Warring States Project, 2017. https://doi.org /10.2307/j.ctvcwpomv.

Häberl, Charles G., and James F. McGrath. *The Mandaean Book of John: Critical Edition, Translation, and Commentary*. Berlin: de Gruyter, 2019. https:// doi.org/10.1515/9783110487862.

Heschel, Abraham J. *The Prophets*. Perennial Classics. New York: HarperCollins, 2001.

Isser, Stanley Jerome. *The Dositheans: A Samaritan Sect in Late Antiquity*. Leiden: Brill, 1976. https://brill.com/view/title/3261.

Jordan, William Chester. "Salome in the Middle Ages." *Jewish History* 26 (2012): 5–15.

Joseph, Simon J. *Jesus, Q, and the Dead Sea Scrolls: A Judaic Approach to Q*. Tübingen: Mohr Siebeck, 2012.

Josephus. *Jewish Antiquities 18–19*. Translated by Louis H. Feldman. Loeb Classical Library. Cambridge, MA: Harvard University Press, 1965.

Kähler, Martin. *The So-Called Historical Jesus and the Historic, Biblical Christ*. Seminar Editions. Philadelphia: Fortress, 1964.

Kateusz, Ally. *Mary and Early Christian Women: Hidden Leadership*. Cham, Switzerland: Springer International, 2019. https://doi.org/10.1007/978-3-030-11111-3.

Knight, Jennifer Lassley. "Herodias, Salomé, and John the Baptist's Beheading." *International Social Science Review* 93 (2017): 1–15.

Kraemer, Ross S. "Implicating Herodias and Her Daughter in the Death of John the Baptizer: A (Christian) Theological Strategy?" *Journal of Biblical Literature* 125 (2006): 321–49. https://doi.org/10.2307/27638363.

Marcus, Joel. *John the Baptist in History and Theology*. Columbia: University of South Carolina Press, 2018.

Marshall, I. Howard. *The Gospel of Luke*. New International Commentary on the New Testament. Grand Rapids: Eerdmans, 1978.

Marshall, Jonathan. *Jesus, Patrons, and Benefactors: Roman Palestine and the Gospel of Luke*. Tübingen: Mohr Siebeck, 2009.

McGrath, James F. "'Destroy This Temple': Issues of History in John 2:13–22." In *Aspects of Historicity in the Fourth Gospel*, edited by Paul N. Anderson, Felix Just, and Tom Thatcher, 35–44. Vol. 2 of *John, Jesus, and History*. Atlanta: Society of Biblical Literature, 2009. https://doi.org/10.2307/j.ctt16ptndz.8.

———. "History and Fiction in the Acts of Thomas: The State of the Question." *Journal for the Study of the Pseudepigrapha* 17 (2008): 297–311. https://doi.org/10.1177/0951820708091899.

McManigal, Daniel W. *A Baptism of Judgment in the Fire of the Holy Spirit: John's Eschatological Proclamation in Matthew 3*. Library of New Testament Studies. London: Bloomsbury, 2019.

Meier, John P. *A Marginal Jew: Rethinking the Historical Jesus*. Vol. 1, *The Roots of the Problem and the Person*. New Haven: Yale University Press, 1991.

Mills, Lynn E., and Nicholas Moore. "One Baptism Once: The Origins of the Unrepeatability of Christian Baptism." *Early Christianity* 11 (2020): 206–26. https://doi.org/10.1628/ec-2020-0015.

Mokhoathi, Joel. "Christian Piety and Pardon: The Vindication of Post-baptismal Sins." *Pharos Journal of Theology* 99 (2018). http://www.pharosjot.com.

Müller, Christoph G. *Mehr als ein Prophet: Die Charakterzeichnung Johannes des Täufers im lukanischen Erzählwerk*. Herders Biblische Studien. Freiburg im Breisgau: Herder, 2001.

Müller, Ulrich B. *Johannes der Täufer: Jüdischer Prophet und Wegbereiter Jesu*. Leipzig: Evangelische Verlagsanstalt, 2002.

Murphy-O'Connor, Jerome. *The Holy Land: An Oxford Archaeological Guide from Earliest Times to 1700*. Oxford Archaeological Guides. Oxford: Oxford University Press, 2008.

———. "Sites Associated with John the Baptist." *Revue biblique* 112 (2005): 265–66.

Orlov, Andrei A. *The Greatest Mirror: Heavenly Counterparts in the Jewish Pseudepigrapha*. Albany: State University of New York Press, 2017.

Robbins, Vernon K. *Who Do People Say I Am? Rewriting Gospel in Emerging Christianity*. Grand Rapids: Eerdmans, 2013.

Ryen, Jon Olav. "Baptism in Jordan—for Christians and Gnostics: Remarkable Similarities between Old Syrian Baptismal Liturgies and the Mandaean Masbuta." *Journal of Ancient Christianity/Zeitschrift für Antikes Christentum* 13 (2009): 282–315. https://doi.org/10.1515/ZAC.2009.20.

Schwartz, Daniel R. "Malthace, Archelaus, and Herod Antipas: Between Genealogy and Typology." In *Sources and Interpretation in Ancient Judaism: Stud-*

ies for Tal Ilan at Sixty, edited by Meron Piotrkowski, Geoffrey Herman, and Saskia Doenitz, 32–40. Leiden: Brill, 2018. https://doi.org/10.1163/9789004366985.

Sebastian, C. D. "Interaction between Classical Indian Ethics and Christian Ethics." In *A Historical-Developmental Study of Classical Indian Philosophy of Morals*, edited by Rajendra Prasad, 477–96. Vol. 12, part 2 of *History of Science, Philosophy, and Culture in Indian Civilization*. New Delhi: Concept, 2009.

Shedd, Nathan L. *A Dangerous Parting: The Beheading of John the Baptist in Early Christian Memory*. Waco, TX: Baylor University Press, 2021.

Stein, Robert H. *Jesus the Messiah: A Survey of the Life of Christ*. Downers Grove, IL: InterVarsity Press, 2009.

Strong, Anise K. *Prostitutes and Matrons in the Roman World*. Cambridge: Cambridge University Press, 2016.

Sundermann, Werner. "What Has Come Down to Us from Manicheism?" In *Light against Darkness: Dualism in Ancient Mediterranean Religion and the Contemporary World*, edited by Armin Lange, Eric M. Meyers, Bennie H. Reynolds III, and Randall Styers, 226–48. Journal of Ancient Judaism Supplements 2. Göttingen: Vandenhoeck & Ruprecht, 2010. https://doi.org/10.13109/9783666550164.226.

Tannous, Jack. *The Making of the Medieval Middle East*. Princeton: Princeton University Press, 2018. https://doi.org/10.23943/princeton/9780691179094.003.0013.

Taylor, David G. K. "The Syriac Baptism of St. John: A Christian Ritual of Protection for Muslim Children." In *The Late Antique World of Early Islam: Muslims among Christians and Jews in the East Mediterranean*, edited by Robert G. Hoyland, 437–60. Berlin: Gerlach, 2021. https://doi.org/10.2307/j.ctv1b9f5mn.21.

Taylor, Joan E. "John the Baptist on the River Jordan: Localities and Their Significance." *ARAM Periodical* 29 (2017): 365–83.

———. "Two by Two: The Ark-Etypal Language of Mark's Apostolic Pairings." In *The Body in Biblical, Christian and Jewish Texts*, edited by Joan E. Taylor, 58–82. Library of Second Temple Studies. London: Bloomsbury T&T Clark, 2014.

Torrance, T. F. "Proselyte Baptism." *New Testament Studies* 1 (1954): 150–54. https://doi.org/10.1017/S0028688500003696.

Turner, John D., trans. "Trimorphic Protennoia." *Gnostic Society Library*. http://
gnosis.org/naghamm/trimorph-JDT.html.

Visi, Tamás. "The Chronology of John the Baptist and the Crucifixion of Jesus
of Nazareth." *Journal for the Study of the Historical Jesus* 18 (2020): 3–34.
https://doi.org/10.1163/17455197-2019003.

Warren, Tish Harrison. "Did Jesus Really Rise from the Dead?" *New York Times*,
April 9, 2023. https://www.nytimes.com/2023/04/09/opinion/jesus-rise
-from-the-dead-easter.html.

Weren, Wim J. C. "Herodias and Salome in Mark's Story about the Beheading of
John the Baptist." *HTS Theological Studies* 75 (2019): art. 5573. https://doi
.org/10.4102/hts.v75i4.5573.

Zangenberg, Jürgen K. "Pure Stone: Archaeological Evidence for Jewish Purity
Practices in Late Second Temple Judaism (Miqwa'ot and Stone Vessels)."
In *Purity and the Forming of Religious Traditions in the Ancient Mediterra-
nean World and Ancient Judaism*, edited by Christian Frevel and Christophe
Nihan, 537–72. Dynamics in the History of Religions 3. Leiden: Brill, 2013.
https://doi.org/10.1163/9789004232297_020.

Index of Subjects

Strong, Anise K., 80n7
Sundermann, Werner, 144n2

Tannous, Jack, 149n7
Taylor, David G. K., 149n7
Taylor, Joan E., 68n1, 78n6
temple, 9, 25–26, 34–46, 50–57; de-
struction of, 110, 114, 135, 145. *See also*
Jesus: temple action and prediction
of its destruction; priesthood;
sacrifice
Theophilus, 2
Tiberias, 126–28, 131, 137–38
Tiberius Caesar, 21n3, 119–20, 127
Torah, 18–19, 22, 41–42, 74, 82n9,
84–85
Turner, John D., 147n6

Visi, Tamás, 53n9

war, 104, 110, 114, 122–23, 127
Weren, Wim J. C., 125n13
Wilde, Oscar, 116
wilderness, 4, 22–24, 27, 44–47, 67–
69, 81–82, 87–88; Israel's wanderings
in, 31–33, 130–32
Wright, N. T., 106n10

Zangenberg, Jürgen K., 39n1
Zechariah, 2, 14–22, 30–31, 33–36, 98,
138; in Islam, 147; as martyr in the
Protevangelium of James, 34, 135, 143

Index of Scripture and Other Ancient Sources

169